Fear Not
I Know Your Name

God's Word for Your Journey to Freedom

Lori Davis

*"You shall know the truth, and the truth
shall make you free."*
John 8:32

Fear Not I Know Your Name

Scripture quotations are from the King James Version of the Bible.

ISBN: 0-9790296-1-9

Published by:

Master Press
318 SE 4th Terrace
Cape Coral, FL. 33990
(800) 325-9136
www.Master-Press.com

Acknowledgments

Without the encouragement of our Lord and His ambassadors, this work would still be a collection of verses handwritten in my daily calendar.

Thank you, Melvin, for your unconditional love, your vision, your encouragement, and for allowing me to work for the Lord.

Camden, my fearless son, I am so proud of you! The Lord has used you to smooth off many rough edges in my life. I can't wait to see all He has planned for you.

Bria, my blessed miracle child, how I enjoy your sense of humor! God knew we needed a compassionate, joyful techie in this world. I'm so thankful He saw fit to give me a place in your life.

Dr. Anne Koci, you are the one who first encouraged me to make this work public. I will forever see your smile and hear your voice reminding me to move onward and upward fulfilling the plans God has for me each day.

Pam Lawson, your hours of reading and editing have finally paid off. You came into my life at the perfect time with an abundance of prayer and encouragement. How grateful I am for your friendship.

Sammye Selecman, you are my teacher, my mentor, and the inspiration for parts II and III of this book. I have never known anyone to be so consumed with the Lord and His work. What an example you have been for me and many others.

Central Baptist Women of the Word, you have loved me, prayed for me, encouraged me, and continue to be attentive as I endeavor to convey what the Lord places on my heart every week. I love you girls!

There are so many others who have walked with me on this journey. May God return your blessings one hundred fold.

CONTENTS

Introduction

Are you gripped by fear? Do you find yourself trying to escape or avoid threatening circumstances? Does apprehension prevent you from accomplishing daily tasks and enjoying everyday life? If so, you are not alone.

Many others, including myself, have at one time or another been bound by the chains of dread, panic, and fear. We have been drawn into the quicksand of defeat by seemingly insurmountable insecurities and anxieties.

Although I was a follower of Christ and had been set free from the fear of death, I allowed the chains of other fears to form a barricade around my life preventing me from moving forward toward the purposes God had for me.

I John 4:18 weighed heavy on my heart: *"There is no fear in love; but perfect love casteth out fear; because fear hath torment. He that feareth is not made perfect in love."*

The Lord gently but firmly began to show me that fear had such a strong hold on me that it had to be replaced with something more powerful. That power came through the daily application of His Word to my life.

I began to read and study everything the Bible had to say about fear and asked God to speak to me personally regarding each scripture passage. As I prayed through the verses, the chains that had me bound began to fall link by link. My fears were replaced by a healthy respect for His majesty and sovereign rule over my life.

The lifeline He held out was only strengthened when I understood God's lovingkindness toward me and my identity in Christ Jesus as explained in the New Testament.

Seeing the change in my life inspired others who were struggling with fear to ask for a copy of the verses I was praying so that they too could be set free. It is a privilege and a joy to now share these powerful truths with you.

I suggest you meditate on one passage per day asking the Lord to apply it to specific areas of your life. Take time to talk with God after you read each selection, then be still and allow Him to respond in your spirit. I've included daily prayers, but I would encourage you to use them only as a starting point. Remember that He longs to spend time with *you* and wants to hear the cry of *your* heart.

PART I

Fear Not

DAY 1

*Psalm 36:7 How excellent is thy **lovingkindness**, O God! Therefore the children of men put their trust under the shadow of thy wings.*

How often have you succeeded at doing something perfectly? Even among world-class athletes there are very few perfect scores ever received. But the Creator of the universe, the Only Wise God, is perfect in all things, including lovingkindness. Lovingkindness is a covenant term. It is a promise that He will always act in ways that are for our benefit. He will always remember us, and will always seek out ways to bless us. What a shadow to rest under!

How thankful I am that there is no flaw in your lovingkindness. I trust you, Lord, to act on my behalf today… (Continue your prayer naming the specific areas of concern.)

DAY 2

*Genesis 15:1 After these things the word of the LORD came unto Abram in a vision, saying, **Fear not**, Abram; I am thy shield, and thy exceeding great reward.*

The first time **"fear not"** is mentioned in the Bible, God gives Abram the reason for this command, "*I am* thy shield**,** and thy exceeding great reward." In whatever situation we as God's covenant partners find ourselves beginning to fear, we must remember that He is our shield. Nothing will come into our lives unless He allows it and knows full well the results. It must be for our good and His glory, or it will be disallowed. Secondly, He promises to be our reward. He would not have us seeking the reward of man because that only brings anxiety into our lives.

Lord, show me the specific areas in my life where I have been seeking the reward of man rather than living to please you. (Give the Lord time to point these out in your life.)

DAY 3

*Proverbs 15:16 Better is little with the **fear of the LORD** than great treasure and trouble therewith.*

Solomon understood that the fear of the LORD was more valuable than any earthly treasure. He could speak from experience because he had known both in his lifetime. What are you seeking in this life…the LORD or great treasure?

Father, knowing you has been the greatest treasure this life could afford. I would never want to exchange the joy of knowing you with even the most luxurious treasure this world has to offer. Show me clearly anything that has concealed your glory in my life.

DAY 4

*Genesis 18:15 Then Sarah denied, saying, I laughed not; for she **was afraid**. And he said, Nay; but thou didst laugh.*

Sarah responded with unbelief to the angels' declaration of her ability to conceive. When she was questioned she denied her skepticism. The scripture plainly tells us what prompted that lie – fear. We have probably all been witnesses to a very similar chain of events in our own lives. Unbelief leads to sin which leads to fear which leads to more sin. What an antagonist fear tends to be. He loves to bring a host of troublemakers to dinner.

Father, help me to accept reproof when it is needed and not exacerbate the situation by trying to cover my transgression with even more sin.

DAY 5

Genesis 21:17 And God heard the voice of the lad; and the angel of God called to Hagar out of heaven, and said unto her, "What aileth thee, Hagar? Fear not; for God hath heard the voice of the lad where he is."

God hears us wherever we are. Resources had seemingly run out, and Hagar put her child under a shrub to die. She walked away so as not to see the death of her child; yet our all-seeing God, El Roi, knew exactly where she and her child were physically, emotionally, and spiritually. He did not desert either one of them. And how did God provide? He opened the mother's eyes to see the resource that would meet the physical need of her child. His provision was close enough for her to see the moment her eyes were opened. Hagar's faith was stabilized and her countenance lifted.

Father, open my eyes to see your provision in this fearful situation. (Journal God's response.)

DAY 6

*Genesis 22:12 And He said, "Lay not thine hand upon the lad, neither do thou any thing unto him: for now I know that thou **fearest God**, seeing thou hast not withheld thy son, thine only son from me."*

When we have put the LORD GOD first place in our lives the evidence will be abundantly clear. We say that He is our Lord, but when He really is our Lord our grip is tight upon Him and much looser upon everything else.

Lord, you have shown me the altar upon which I must be a living sacrifice. I can identify with the apostle Paul who said that his spirit was willing, but his flesh was weak. I need your assistance moment by moment to remain a pure and holy sacrifice unto you, loosening my selfish grip upon the things you have put within my care. (He knows what they are, but you may need to write them down for your own benefit.)

DAY 7

*Genesis 26:24 And the LORD appeared unto him the same night, and said, I am God of Abraham thy father: **fear not**, for I am with thee, and will bless thee, and multiply thy seed for my servant Abraham's sake.*

Once again a promise from the Great I AM. "*I am* with thee." Jehovah Shammah—the LORD is there. We serve the Omnipresent God who created this universe we live in. There is not a corner hidden from His sight. There is absolutely no spot on this earth that we, His children, can go apart from Him. He not only told Isaac that He was with him but that the covenant made with his father, Abraham, would be fulfilled in all aspects. In other words, "I am with thee and will be with thee to fulfill all the promises I have made to you and your descendents."

Thank you, Father, for being with me even when I doubt....

DAY 8

Genesis 35:17 And it came to pass, when she was in hard labor, that the midwife said unto her, **Fear not***; thou shalt have this son also.*

In the midst of childbearing, Rachael's midwife remembers what she heard Rachael say after Joseph was born, *"God shall give me another child."* The midwife now assures her that God will follow through. This proved to be the end of Rachel's life on this earth, but we are reminded even at the time of our soul's departing to **fear not** because God has His plans all arranged and will continue to keep His promises even when we are not on the earth to see them fulfilled.

Thank you, LORD, that the extent of your promises goes beyond the limit of my physical life. I trust you to deal with _____ _____in your perfect time.

DAY 9

Genesis 43:23 And he said, "Peace be to you, **fear not***: your God, and the God of your father, hath given you treasure in your sacks: I had your money." And he brought Simeon out unto them.*

Peace in place of fear... Oh, the promises of God's eternal Word! When the odds seem stacked against us we must remember that God is our provider, and in the midst of famine can give us treasure in our sacks.

Jehovah Jireh, my provider, how often you have placed treasure in my sack, and still I have a propensity to fear. Forgive me for being ungrateful. All I have needed you have abundantly provided. (Name some of those God-placed treasures.)

DAY 10

Genesis 46:3 And he said, I am God, the God of thy father: **fear not** *to go down into Egypt; for I will there make of thee a great nation:* Once again, *"**I am God**, the God of thy father."*

What did that mean to Jacob? The same God who had been faithful through all of His promises in the past would continue to be faithful in the future. Jacob was acknowledging God at this point in his life and God was directing his paths. There are times when we are called to step out of our comfortable places so that God can do a great work in not only our lives but also in the lives of our future generations. This great blessing often comes through what we fear.

Where is it you would have me go today, Lord? I'll need you to go before me and behind me and still walk beside me to hold my hand. I don't want to hinder your plan for me or for others because of needless anxiety. (Make a note of what He speaks to your spirit.)

DAY 11

*Psalm 89:30-35 If his children forsake my law, and walk not in my judgments; If they break my statutes, and keep not my commandments; Then will I visit their transgression with the rod, and their iniquity with stripes. Nevertheless my **lovingkindness** will I not utterly take from him, nor suffer my faithfulness to fail. My covenant will I not break, nor alter the thing that is gone out of my lips. Once have I sworn by my holiness that I will not lie unto David.*

Discipline is a very important aspect of lovingkindness; it is a covenant blessing. Because God loves us and knows what is best for us He will set boundaries around our lives for protection. Even though those boundaries may feel like an electric fence at times, we do well to keep in mind that the power source is God's jealous love for us running through cords of covenant.

I have learned, Father, so much about the way you love me through discipline. You are not willing to let me wander away from your covenant. Your commandments and statutes are for my benefit and yet my flesh often fights against them. Thank you for your steadfast determination and consistency in my life. (Continue to journal your prayers and God's tender response in your spirit each day. They will become spiritual markers. Your Creator enjoys spending time with you!)

DAY 12

*Genesis 50:19 And Joseph said unto them, **Fear not**: for am I in the place of God?*

One who exhibits Christ's character reminds us that it is God and not man that we must fear. Regardless of our fear of what man may do to us, even as a result of our own misconduct, it is God who is ultimately in control.

Lord, have I allowed anyone or anything to take your position in my life? Once again, I place you on the throne.

DAY 13

*Genesis 50:21 Now therefore **fear ye not**: I will nourish you, and your little ones. And he comforted them, and spake kindly unto them.*

Our nourishment in times of great need is already planned by our Heavenly Father. What comfort to those of us who are as undeserving as Joseph's brothers. Joseph's actions certainly exhibit what it means to *trust in the LORD and do good* when faced with evildoers (Psalm 37:1-6).

As I commit my way to you, Lord, I trust you, knowing that you have already gone before me and prepared the way.

DAY 14

*Psalm 40:11 Withhold not thou thy tender mercies from me, O LORD: let thy **lovingkindness** and thy truth continually preserve me.*

When we come to the throne of grace not only do we find grace, but mercy with it as well. It is not a reluctant and rigid mercy, but a tender mercy which desires that we reciprocate by giving the same to others. That's why He preserves us, so that His mercy can ooze out of us.

When a preservative is used, the object which would have otherwise been rotten often takes on some characteristics of that which has preserved it. Oh that my life would take on the character of your lovingkindness and truth!

DAY 15

*Psalm 40:10 I have not hid thy righteousness within my heart; I have declared thy faithfulness and thy salvation: I have not concealed thy **lovingkindness** and thy truth from the great congregation.*

Our Lord does not show us lovingkindness so that we can sit and soak in it. No! He wants us to share our story with others so that the whole world might know that He is God.

As I declare your faithfulness, Lord, use my words and my actions in such a way that others will desire also to serve you and be partakers of your lovingkindness.

DAY 16

*Exodus 1:17 But the midwives **feared God**, and did not as the king of Egypt commanded them, but saved the men children alive.*

We must keep in mind that as Christians we have a dual citizenship. We are to obey the authority that has been placed over us on this earth unless it comes into conflict with our higher authority. If such a conflict arises, we must prayerfully make a decision, being careful not to allow our personal disposition to interfere with biblical conviction.

Realizing that I have a citizenship both on earth and in heaven, I submit myself to you above all other authority. If the need arises to respectfully disagree with my authorities here, I trust that you will give me the strength and wisdom to do so in a way that will honor you.

DAY 17

*Exodus 14:13 And Moses said unto the people, **Fear ye not**, stand still, and see the salvation of the LORD, which He will show to you today: for the Egyptians whom ye have seen today, ye shall see them again no more forever.*

Stand still and see the salvation of the LORD! If God has brought you into a tight place where it seems there is no escape, you can *be still and know that He is God*; and He will show Himself mighty on your behalf. The enemy that seems overpowering today may be of no consequence tomorrow.

Father, this enemy seems bigger than life, and yet you tell me you can eliminate him forever. Help me to see today's trials from your perspective so that I can stand still and watch you work.

DAY 18

Philippians 4:6-8 Be careful [anxious] for nothing; but in every thing by prayer and supplication with thanksgiving let your requests be made known unto God. ⁷ And the peace of God, which passeth all understanding, shall keep your hearts and minds through Christ Jesus. ⁸ Finally, brethren, whatsoever things are true, whatsoever things are honest, whatsoever things are just, whatsoever things are pure, whatsoever things are lovely, whatsoever things are of good report; if there be any virtue, and if there be any praise, think on these things.

What am I to do while being still before Him? Meditate on those things mentioned in Paul's letter to the church at Philippi. This is definitely a passage that should be stored in the memory so as to filter all your thoughts.

Thank you, Lord, for this wonderful promise concerning my thought life. Help me to quickly recognize when I am thinking outside of these parameters.

DAY 19

*Exodus 20:19-21 And they said unto Moses, Speak thou with us, and we will hear: but let not God speak with us, lest we die. ²⁰ And Moses said unto the people, **Fear not**: for God is come to prove you, and that his fear may be before your faces, that ye sin not. ²¹ And the people stood afar off, and Moses drew near unto the thick darkness where God was.*

The children of Israel expose a perfect example of misdirected fear that leads to sin and bondage. They feared death, which created an ungodly separation. Moses, however, had a healthy fear of the Lord and drew near to the Father. *(Psalm 4:4, 5 Tremble and do not sin; Meditate in your heart upon your bed, and be still. Offer the sacrifices of righteousness, and trust in the LORD.)*

Oh how often I have allowed anxiety transport me to places you would not have had me go! It has disturbed my peace and disrupted my love. You can handle this in a way that will be redemptive. Help me to hand it over.

DAY 20

*Leviticus 25:17 Ye shall not therefore oppress one another; but thou shalt **fear thy God**; for I am the LORD your God.*

A deep reverence and awe for our Holy God will produce in us a desire to treat others as He Himself would treat them.

LORD, is there anyone in my life that I have oppressed, knowingly or inadvertently? How would you have me to show them your kindness and gentleness?

DAY 21

*Leviticus 25:43 Thou shalt not rule over him with rigor; but shalt **fear thy God**.*

God alone is the ruler. We must be ever mindful of the fact that we are servant leaders, reverencing the LORD our God in all our dealings with others.

I realize, Lord, that all authorities that exist are established by you, and are to be ministers for you. I need help to submit to those authorities you have set over me and also to serve your purposes where you have placed me in leadership positions.

DAY 22

Numbers 12:8 With him will I speak mouth to mouth, even apparently, and not in dark speeches; and the similitude of the LORD shall he behold: wherefore then were ye not afraid to speak against my servant Moses?

Along with the fear of the LORD comes a respect for his servants. When Miriam and Aaron offended Moses, God took it personally and they were dealt with severely. We should remember from this example that it is a very dangerous thing to speak against or be disrespectful to any of God's servants.

Put a guard over the doorpost of my mouth, Father, and let me not disregard the instruction that you have given to another.

DAY 23

*Numbers 14:9 Only rebel not ye against the LORD, neither fear ye the people of the land; for they are bread for us: their defense is departed from them, and the LORD is with us: **fear** them **not**.*

Who is with you? And where is the defense of your enemy? The LORD admonishes us through his servants, Joshua and Caleb, not to fear the people who seem to stand in the way of His blessings. We are also reminded not to rebel against the One who is our shield and defender. Our rebellion could easily become our worst enemy.

Father, the world is clamoring for my attention, but I know that the Son of God in me should be about my Father's business. It would be rebellion on my part to allow a fear or reverence of the world around me to overshadow my reverence of and obedience to you. Help me to be steadfast.

DAY 24

*Psalm 107:43 Whoso is wise, and will observe these things, even they shall understand the **lovingkindness** of the LORD.*

This entire Psalm is worth your reading today. The writer describes a range of distresses that God's people found themselves in as a result of rebellion. However, when *"they cried out to the LORD in their trouble, He delivered them out of their distresses."* Each stanza speaks of God's lovingkindness, or covenant loyalty, which is everlasting.

Your Word, O LORD, has been written for our instruction, and how applicable it is in this day when men are wandering in the wilderness, dwelling in darkness, foolishness, rebelliousness, and depending on earthly pleasures for happiness. It is my desire this day to walk in the wisdom of your Word and not in the wisdom of the world. Help me to understand lovingkindness.

DAY 25

*Numbers 21:34 And the LORD said unto Moses, "**Fear him not**: for I have delivered him into thy hand, and all his people, and his land; and thou shalt do to him as thou didst unto Sihon king of the Amorites, which dwelt at Heshbon.*

God reminds Moses of past victories as He assures him that this giant and all his people have already been slated for defeat.

We need not fear the giants in our lives or their cohorts whom God has already defeated on our behalf.

Thank you, Jehovah Sabaoth, Lord of Hosts, for past, present, and future victories.

DAY 26

*Deuteronomy 1:17 Ye shall not respect persons in judgment; but ye shall hear the small as well as the great; **ye shall not be afraid** of the face of man; for the judgment is God's; and the cause that is too hard for you, bring it to me and I will hear it.*

When Moses appointed judges of the people he admonished them to be impartial and to hear both sides carefully and completely regardless of who is receiving the judgment. Why? We are God's stewards, acting on behalf of the most just judge whom we must not misrepresent.

I have been tempted to be partial out of respect or disrespect for particular people or because of the fear of retribution. If I am to show forth your character, those thoughts must never again enter my mind in judgment. Remind me, Lord.

DAY 27

*Deuteronomy 1:21 Behold, the LORD thy God hath set the land before thee: go up and possess it, as the LORD God of thy fathers hath said unto thee; **fear not**, neither be discouraged.*

Be aware, God has given you an inheritance; go in and occupy it. Don't be discouraged by what you see with your eyes. Jehovah, the great I AM, has promised to be completing the work He began in you until the day of Christ Jesus.

Lord, I am your child, and I should not be known as one who shrinks back at the first sign of crisis. I want my life to show forth your faithfulness. Help me to be confident and bold in possessing what you have already purchased for me.

DAY 28
*Deuteronomy 1:29 Dread not, **neither be afraid** of them.*

Dreading what could come to pass causes more stress in our lives than what actually does come to pass. Our Lord wants to free us from this unnecessary encumbrance. The key is TRUST: **T**otally **R**elying **U**nder **S**tressful **T**endencies.

You have earned my confidence, Father. There is no reason that I should question your ability to reroute the enemy or give me strength and wisdom during the battle. I hand over all those things I've been dreading with full confidence that you are more than capable of preparing me for what is ahead.

DAY 29
*Deuteronomy 3:2 And the LORD said unto me, **Fear** him **not**: for I will deliver him, and all his people, and his land, into thy hand; and thou shalt do unto him as thou didst unto Sihon king of the Amorites, which dwelt at Heshbon.*

Moses rehearses God's faithfulness. We must remember that God can deal with the giants in our lives as though they were grasshoppers. No man's power can protect him from God Almighty.

You, Lord, are a God of complete deliverance. You did not deliver me only partially from my sin, and I trust that you will not deliver me only partially from the fears that often overtake me. I know it will require my full cooperation if the evil one is to be defeated in my life.

DAY 30

*Psalm 36:10 O continue thy **lovingkindness** unto them that know thee; and thy righteousness to the upright in heart.*

A correct knowledge of God will lead to a correct attitude of the heart. David knew that it was God's lovingkindness that had preserved his life thus far, and only through this covenant promise would he be sustained.

What right do I have asking you to continue to be as good to me as you have always been? I have no right at all except what you purchased for me by your own blood. I have yielded my rights to you as best as I know how, and you have given me more in return than I would have ever dreamed.

DAY 31

*Deuteronomy 3:22 Ye shall **not fear** them: for the LORD your God he shall fight for you.*

The question I must ask myself is, "Am I depending on my own methods and manipulations or on my Sovereign Lord?"

For years I have tried to fight these battles on my own. I have discovered that when I start pulling strings I am only unraveling the perfect tapestry of trust you have so beautifully been preparing in my life. It is my desire, Father, to no longer weave stray threads in that tapestry or miss the full impact of your creative work because of my impatience and fear.

DAY 32

*Deuteronomy 7:18 Thou shalt **not be afraid** of them: but shalt well remember what the LORD thy God did unto Pharaoh, and unto all Egypt.*

To remember means to bring to mind or think of again; to keep in mind for attention or consideration. God wants us to engage our minds when fear is approaching. And notice He says to remember well. That means to recall the details. How has God delivered you in the past? What did He do that could be attributed to no man? Keep this in your mind and consider it often.

Thank you, Lord, for past victories. No matter how awesome the task may seem, or how massive the enemy looms, my trust is based on your unchanging nature.

DAY 33

*Isaiah 63:7 I will mention the **lovingkindnesses** of the LORD, and the praises of the LORD, according to all that* *the LORD hath bestowed on us, and the great goodness toward the house of Israel, which he hath bestowed on them according to his mercies, and according to the multitude of his **lovingkindnesses**.*

God's lovingkindnesses are multiple. There is much to praise Him for. Take a look back over your own life and see if He has not been abundant in lovingkindness. Then follow Isaiah's example and tell others about the goodness and mercy of your God.

The fact that you would choose to give me life still amazes me, Lord. You knew that my actions would often cause you pain and yet you gave life to me and then drew me into your family. May my mouth be an instrument of praise and blessing as I mention your lovingkindness throughout this day.

DAY 34

*Deuteronomy 10:12, 13 And now, Israel, what doth the LORD thy God require of thee, but to **fear the LORD thy God**, to walk in all his ways, and to love him, and to serve the LORD thy God with all thy heart and with all thy soul, To keep the commandments of the LORD, and his statutes, which I command thee this day for thy good?*

Just as the chosen ones of the Old Covenant were given this assignment for their good, we too are given the same command under the New Covenant. Jesus boiled it down to loving God and loving others. There are many examples of those who refused to follow this command. If we learn from their mistakes, we'll not have to make them ourselves.

Father, it is not always simple to walk in your ways, but I understand the necessity. It is a joy to love you and serve you. Thank you for clearly marking the pathway within Your Word and for the promises that apply to our obedience.

DAY 35

*Deuteronomy 13:4 Ye shall walk after the LORD your God, and **fear Him**, and keep His commandments, and obey His voice, and ye shall serve Him, and cleave unto Him.*

This particular chapter contains numerous warnings concerning idolatry and divination. The standard of truth in your life must never be signs, wonders or someone else's experience, but the Word of God. Notice the action words in this verse: walk, fear, keep, obey, serve, and cleave. If you are following this order idolatry will not be a problem.

Father, you began cultivating this reverential fear in me long before I realized your involvement in my life. I desire to continue walking in obedience, service, and the constant cleaving that prevents the wedge of idolatry.

DAY 36

*Deuteronomy 18:22 When a prophet speaketh in the name of the LORD, if the thing follow not, nor come to pass, that is the thing which the LORD hath not spoken, but the prophet hath spoken it presumptuously: thou shalt **not be afraid** of him.*

Just as we are called to respect God's servants, we are called to be cautious about those who claim to be of God and offer no proof. Hebrews 1:2 reminds us that *in these last days God has spoken to us in His Son.* There is no new information coming. If you can't find it in THE BOOK, it is not to be feared.

Lord, give me a discerning heart so that I can readily identify those who are of you as opposed to those who desire to lead us with their own agenda.

DAY 37

Deuteronomy 20:1 When you go out to battle against your enemies and see horses and chariots and people more numerous than you, **do not be afraid** *of them; for the LORD your God, who brought you up from the land of Egypt, is with you.*

It is often the things we see and hear that frighten us. Our God may be invisible to our sight, but He is ever-present, in full battle array, as our commander-in-chief.

Starting the day without my marching orders makes me want to retreat or wave the white flag because I'm sizing up the situation according to my own senses. However, when I report to you for my instructions first thing in the morning, you are gracious to remind me of your presence which is more valuable than all the enemy's resources. Please continue to interject your plans into my thought processes so as to overrule my own.

DAY 38

Deuteronomy 20:3,4 And shall say unto them, Hear, O Israel, ye approach this day unto battle against your enemies: let not your hearts faint, **fear not,** *and do not tremble, neither be ye* *terrified because of them: For the LORD your God is He that goeth with you, to fight for you against your enemies, to save you.*

Notice that fear affects not only our mind but also our physical body. As difficult situations arise we must remember to allow our Shield and Defender to protect all aspects of our being and do the fighting for us. What happens when God does the defending? He saves us!

Lord, take over my mind, will, physical body, and emotions so that when trouble arrives I neither faint, tremble, fear, nor panic. May your calmness invade every aspect of my being so that I honor you at all times.

DAY 39

*Deuteronomy 31:6 Be strong and of a good courage, **fear not**, nor be afraid of them: for the LORD thy God, he it is that doth go with thee; he will not fail thee, nor forsake thee.*

I am only the armor bearer for the LORD my God. I can be courageous as long as it is He who is with me. He will never turn His back, abandon, neglect, or desert me, even in times of danger.

Lord, when you are with me, perfect love is with me and perfect love casts out fear. I have much to learn about perfect love, the love that will not abandon, neglect or desert, even when circumstances are threatening. Teach me gently, Lord.

DAY 40

*Psalm 138:2 I will worship toward thy holy temple, and praise thy name for thy **lovingkindness** and for thy truth: for thou hast magnified thy word above all thy name.*

Praise is an integral part of worship. And what better gift to bring before the throne than thanksgiving for God's steadfast love and constant truth. The truth of God's Word stands together with the faithfulness of His name. Because His name will never fail, neither will His Word.

It is because of your truth that I can make it through even the most difficult days. Your promises to be with me and act on my behalf have been confirmed over and over again.

DAY 41

*Deuteronomy 31:8 And the LORD, He it is that doth go before thee; He will be with thee, He will not fail thee, neither forsake thee: **fear not**, neither be dismayed.*

As Moses hands over the baton of leadership to Joshua, he reminds the children of Israel that it is not a man they are following. A man could not promise to never leave and never forsake them. It is Jehovah, the covenant keeping God, whom the enemy encounters before he is able to approach you.

I have a tendency to allow people to occupy pedestals in my life that only you should fill. It is you that has been working through them to love me, teach me, and help me. I want no man or woman to ever be exalted above you in my life.

DAY 42

*Joshua 1:9 Have not I commanded thee? Be strong and of a good courage; **be not afraid**, neither be thou dismayed: for the LORD thy God is with thee whithersoever thou goest.*

This is not the first time God gave this admonition and it will not be the last. He is very serious about this command and expects complete obedience.

First time obedience is what I expect from my children, Father, and I assume that you expect no less. I realize that wherever I go today you are with me. The way I react to the situations you allow in my life will either honor you and your kingdom or bring dishonor to your name. I choose to take the courage you provide and move forward to esteem you.

DAY 43

*Joshua 8:1 And the LORD said unto Joshua, **Fear not**, neither be thou dismayed; take all the people of war with thee, and arise, go up to Ai; see, I have given into thy hand the king of Ai, and his people, and his city, and his land:*

The children of Israel had been defeated at Ai because there was sin in the camp. The sin had been dealt with and God encouraged Joshua to go forward in victory. We must not let the enemy remind us of past failures in order to deprive us of future victories. *"God's mercies are new every morning."*

How often the enemy brings up my past failures! Why? To deprive me of future victory! I'll have no more of that. If you supply new mercy to me every morning, I will take it and offer it to others also.

DAY 44

Lamentations 3:21-24 This I recall to my mind, therefore have I hope. It is of the LORD's mercies that we are not consumed, because his compassions fail not. They are new every morning: great is thy faithfulness. The LORD is my portion, saith my soul; therefore will I hope in him.

In the midst of Jeremiah's deep turmoil, he acknowledges that there is still reason to hope: God's mercies, lovingkindnesses, will never cease. We may open ourselves up to the horrible consequences of sin, but in the midst of the discipline we must remember that His pain was much greater than we can know. And He remains faithful.

Without your mercy, Lord, I would have been consumed; without your compassion I could not look up. I have hope only because you are faithful, so I will trust you once again.

DAY 45

*Joshua 10:8 And the LORD said unto Joshua, **Fear them not**: for I have delivered them into thine hand; there shall not a man of them stand before thee.*

Joshua was called on to honor a covenant that he had made without seeking the counsel of the LORD. The consequences were long term, but God did not leave Joshua because of his impulsiveness. God remained faithful and still honored His promise never to forsake His children.

Lord, we humans tend to make covenants without thinking them through very carefully. You were faithful to help Joshua fulfill the responsibilities of an unwise covenant. Give me strength to follow through with my obligations even when they are unpleasant. I know you can bring good even from my bad choices.

DAY 46

*Joshua 10:25 And Joshua said unto them, **Fear not,** nor be dismayed, be strong and of good courage: for thus shall the LORD do to all your enemies against whom ye fight.*

God had just increased Israel's faith by once again defeating a formidable enemy. As the Israelite chiefs stood on the necks of the five Amorite kings, Joshua echoes the promise God made to him at the onset of his calling. All of our enemies are also under the feet of Jesus (Psalm 110:1).

I too, Father, desire to be confident in sharing your promises, knowing that you watch over your Word to perform it.

DAY 47

*Joshua 11:6 And the LORD said unto Joshua, **Be not afraid** because of them; for tomorrow about this time will I deliver them up all slain before Israel: thou shalt hough their horses, and burn their chariots with fire.*

A multitude as great as the sand on the seashore rallied to fight against God's people. The odds were stacked against them, but our God does not operate according to the odds. He Himself promised to deliver the enemy into the hand of Israel, and this He did: *"there was not any left to breathe."*

Thank you, Mighty God, for past, present, and future deliverance in my life. I need to be reminded that the only true danger is being outside of your will.

DAY 48

*Psalm 17:7 Shew thy marvelous **lovingkindness**, O thou that savest by thy right hand them which put their trust in thee from those that rise up against them.*

A very important aspect of covenant is that one would use all of his resources to protect a covenant partner from his enemies. David had no doubt that God's covenant love would cause Him to respond in power when the enemy began an insurgence.

Almighty God, Jehovah-Sabaoth, I call upon you this day to show your lovingkindness and respond on my behalf towards the enemy who desires to cause devastation in my life. I submit myself to your right hand of power and stand dressed in the weapons of warfare (Ephesians 6:10-18) which you so generously supply. (See Appendix A)

DAY 49

*Psalm 42:8 Deep calleth unto deep at the noise of thy waterspouts: all thy waves and thy billows are gone over me. Yet the LORD will command his **lovingkindness** in the daytime, and in the night his song shall be with me, and my prayer unto the God of my life.*

The Psalmist is in turmoil here, yet he acknowledges that God is not out of reach. No matter how deep the flood waters become, God's lovingkindness is our life preserver. No storm can wash away your song or your prayer if Jehovah is your God.

How wonderful the vision of your holiness against the backdrop of a storm tossed sea, and how welcome the light of your steadfast love when the darkness tries to envelope me.

DAY 50
Judges 6:10 And I said unto you, I am the LORD your God; **fear not** *the gods of the Amorites, in whose land ye dwell; but ye have not obeyed my voice.*

Israel was experiencing consequences of disobedience. We must remember that God's "fear not" is a command we must obey. Disobedience always brings destruction.

Show me specific instances, LORD, when I have been disobedient through fear.

DAY 51
Judges 6:23 And the LORD said unto him, Peace be unto thee; **fear not***; thou shalt not die.*

When Gideon realized that he was in the presence of Almighty God, he was awestruck. When we stand in awe of His presence, He assures us of His peace.

Holy God, as I come before your throne, I ask for that same peace to be unto me of which you spoke to your servant Gideon.

DAY 52

*Judges 6:27 Then Gideon took ten men of his servants, and did as the LORD had said unto him: and so it was, because he **feared** his father's household, and the men of the city, that he could not do it by day, that he did it by night.*

After their personal encounter, God instructed Gideon to pull down the altar of Baal that belonged to his father and replace it with an altar to the LORD. Gideon had not yet released all of his fears to the LORD because he decided to do this at night while the city was sleeping. But God proved faithful, and Gideon was even exonerated by his father. Now he was ready for an even bigger task.

Lord, as I release my fears to you one by one, I realize that you are going to test me while proving that you are trustworthy. Give me strength to remove all the altars to the god of fear in my life.

DAY 53

*Ruth 3:11 And now, my daughter, **fear not**; I will do to thee all that thou requirest; for all the city of my people doth know that thou art a virtuous woman.*

Ruth was a virtuous woman. Her reputation as well as her sustenance was in the hands of her kinsman redeemer, and she was not disappointed. Our kinsman redeemer will also do all that is required and more on our behalf.

I so often need to be reminded, Lord, that if I keep my eyes upon you and walk in obedience, you will manage my reputation. Thank you.

DAY 54

*1 Samuel 12:14 If ye will **fear the LORD**, and serve Him, and obey His voice, and not rebel against the cammandment of the LORD, then shall both ye and also the king that reigneth over you continue following the LORD your God:*

The people had asked for a king, and Saul was chosen. But that was not God's best for the nation of Israel. Samuel is reminding Israel of God's standard for obedience, of which they had already fallen short. His standards have not changed. The fear of the LORD involves our total response to Him, not just mental or spiritual participation. If you are not walking in obedience you are walking in rebellion.

Show me, Lord, any point of rebellion that remains in my body, soul, or spirit. I know it is necessary to release that to you.

DAY 55

*I Samuel 12:20 And Samuel said unto the people, **Fear not**: ye have done all this wickedness; yet turn not aside from following the LORD, but serve the LORD with all your heart...*

The sin had been committed, and the people knew they were on a destructive path. However, we serve a God of redemption who hears us as soon as we cry out to Him with all sincerity, willing to repent. He will be with us even in the consequences.

Thank you, Father, for giving your wisdom without reproach (James 1:5).

DAY 56

Psalm 25:6-7 Remember, O LORD, thy tender mercies and thy **lovingkindnesses***; for they have been ever of old. Remember not the sins of my youth, nor my transgressions: according to thy mercy remember thou me for thy goodness' sake, O LORD.*

We would do well to follow David's example in this Psalm. While asking for mercy he acknowledges his personal sin. It is because of God's goodness, not our merit, that He looks at us through lenses of lovingkindness.

It is so outside the parameter of my thinking that you would look at me and recall to mind your personal attributes rather than my sin. Even though I am unable to grasp the scope of it, I stand under the fountain and drink from your abundance.

DAY 57

I Samuel 22:23 Abide thou with me, **fear not***: for he that seeketh my life seeketh thy life: but with me thou shalt be in safeguard.*

David speaks these words of reassurance to Abiathar after Saul ordered the slaying of eighty-five priests. The world is at odds with Jesus Christ. Since He experienced ill treatment, we can expect much of the same. Choosing to abide with Him is most assuredly an eternal safeguard.

I choose to abide with you, Jesus. I know that it will sometimes involve carrying a cross, but never alone.

DAY 58

*I Samuel 23:17 And he said unto him, **Fear not**: for the hand of Saul my father shall not find thee; and thou shalt be king over Israel, and I shall be next unto thee; and that also Saul my father knoweth.*

Even God's chosen king needed to be reminded of God's promises. And our Lord is faithful to send encouragement at the perfect time. These would prove to be Jonathan's last words to David, his covenant friend.

Father, who would you have me to encourage with a "fear not" from your Word today?

DAY 59

*II Samuel 9:7 And David said to him, **Fear not**; for I will surely show thee kindness for Jonathan thy father's sake, and will restore to thee all the land of Saul thy father; and thou shalt eat bread at my table continually.*

We can certainly identify with Mephibosheth, Jonathan's crippled son, who was hiding from David after his father's death. God has searched us out, not to bring condemnation, but in order to give us an eternal inheritance for the sake of His Son. We are restored and the bread is supplied at His table continually.

The kindness you have shown me has been so undeserved, and the bread with which you have fed me has been the perfect sustenance.

DAY 60

*Psalm 26:3 For thy **lovingkindness** is before mine eyes: and I have walked in thy truth.*

David used God's example of lovingkindness as a plumb line and measured his actions according to God's truth rather than man's logic.

As your ambassador in this world, I desire to represent you well. Search my heart, and show me where I have fallen short in my dealings with people.

DAY 61

*Psalm 63:3-6 Because thy **lovingkindness** is better than life, my lips shall praise thee. Thus will I bless thee while I live: I will lift up my hands in thy name. My soul shall be satisfied as with marrow and fatness; and my mouth shall praise thee with joyful lips: When I remember thee upon my bed, and meditate on thee in the night watches.*

This Psalm was given birth in the wilderness of Judah. Notice David's priorities in the midst of his wilderness experience: *thy lovingkindness is better than life. I will bless thee while I live.* In actuality, there would be no life without God's lovingkindness, so it is only right that we bless Him for the life we have been given, even when the darkness surrounds us.

It is true that perfect peace comes when my mind is stayed upon you. It is my desire, Lord, to meditate upon your goodness rather than upon my difficulties.

DAY 62

*I Kings 17:13 And Elijah said to her, **Fear not**; go and do as thou hast said: but make me a little cake from it first, and bring it to me, and then make one for thee and thy son.*

Elijah was God's messenger to the widow. Notice that we may be given a task to prove our heart. Our obedience often precedes God's provision.

You first, Father, others second, and myself last. That would eliminate those fears that are born in my selfish heart.

DAY 63

*II Kings 1:15 And the angel of the LORD said unto Elijah, Go down with him: **be not afraid** of him. And he arose, and went down with him unto the king.*

Has God asked you to speak boldly on His behalf to someone who is in authority over you? Then do so with humble respect, keeping in mind that you represent the King of kings.

Lord, give me boldness when I am hesitant to follow through with your instructions. I realize that I am only useful as long as I allow you to do your work through me. It is when I feel like I've done a great job for you that I am really of no use at all.

DAY 64

*II Kings 6:16 And he answered, **Fear not**: for they that be with us are more than they that be with them.*

In this instance, a servant was in fear because of the enemy that he could see surrounding the city. Elisha asked God to open the servant's eyes in order to behold God's unseen army. God did so, and the servant was able to see a mountain full of God's horses and chariots of fire surrounding Elisha.

Father, help me to live above "see level" trusting that you are doing things I could never imagine.

DAY 65

Romans 8:31 What shall we then say to these things? If God be for us, who can be against us?

I have heard it said many times that there is no safer place than in the center of God's will. No matter the outside objections, God is for you, and as the sovereign ruler of all the universe, He controls what comes near.

So much of life is about trusting you, Lord. I will at times be condemned by man, and there may be false charges brought against me. You have told me to expect tribulation, and persecution, but I cling to the reminder that none of these things can separate me from your love.

DAY 66

*II Kings 17:7 For so it was, that the children of Israel had sinned against the LORD their God, which had brought them up out of the land of Egypt, from under the hand of Pharaoh king of Egypt, and had **feared** other gods.*

Where did this fear of other gods take the children of Israel? The fear took them into captivity. They had compromised, honoring the gods of the very nations that God had driven from the land of Canaan. Having been warned on many occasions about this practice, they now suffered the consequences. Has compromise led to captivity in any area of your life?

For my entire life, Lord, you have been proving yourself as the One True God. I realize that the things of this world can very easily hold me captive if I begin to compromise in the areas of which you have warned me. Help me, Lord, to maintain my focus.

DAY 67

I Peter 2:19, 20 For this is thankworthy, if a man for conscience toward God endure grief, suffering wrongfully. For what glory is it if, when ye be buffeted for your faults, ye shall take it patiently? But if, when ye do well, and suffer for it, ye take it patiently, this is acceptable with God.

It is good to ask ourselves and the Lord, in the midst of suffering, if we are being disciplined. If our lives line up with His will as expressed in His Word and He gives us no indication of discipline, then we must listen carefully and remain as close to Him as possible. On the other hand, if we are being disciplined, Psalm 51 is a great place to get insight into true repentance and restoration.

I have suffered on both fronts, Lord, and I thank you for quickly showing me the areas of rebellion that have brought grief into my own life. I have found that the solution for both sources of pain is to get as close to you as possible. Thank you for never turning me away.

DAY 68

*II Kings 17:25 And so it was at the beginning of their dwelling there, that they **feared not the LORD**: therefore the LORD sent lions among them, which slew some of them.*

The king of Assyria brought ungodly people in to occupy the land after the Israelites were carried away into exile. These new citizens were not to prosper there either because they worshiped many gods. God is the blessed controller of all things, and He can use even animals to do His bidding.

I know that eventually, Father, all who do not acknowledge you as the One True God will greatly regret their omission. Thank you for the assurance that you are the blessed controller even if you must prompt the animals to do your bidding.

DAY 69

*II Kings 17:35 With whom the LORD had made a covenant and charged them, saying, Ye shall **not fear** other gods, nor bow yourselves to them, nor serve them, nor sacrifice to them:*

I must constantly ask myself, "Who or what am I serving? Whom do I fear? To whom do I bow myself down or sacrifice for?" If the answer is not the LORD GOD who made heaven and earth, I must readjust my life and honor my covenant with the One who gave His life for me.

Where do I need readjustment today? Has my allegiance to you grown cold in any area? Search my heart, O God!

DAY 70

*Psalm 51:1-3 Have mercy upon me, O God, according to thy **lovingkindness**: according unto the multitude of thy tender mercies blot out my transgressions. Wash me thoroughly from mine iniquity, and cleanse me from my sin. For I acknowledge my transgressions: and my sin is ever before me.*

The operative words in these verses are "wash me, cleanse me," and "I acknowledge my transgressions." Our covenant God is generous with His mercy, but only if we acknowledge and repent of our offenses toward Him.

Lord and Savior Jesus Christ, you are the one who is able to present me faultless before the throne. I know that if it were my life being evaluated in order to enter God's presence I would be rejected. Thank you for living a pure life on my behalf and taking my place in death. I have certainly been a recipient of your boundless tender mercies.

DAY 71

*II Kings 17:37 And the statutes, and the ordinances, and the law, and the commandment, which He wrote for you, ye shall observe to do for evermore; and ye shall **not fear** other gods.*

The One True God is sovereign and has our best interests at heart in all things. When we are walking in obedience, there is no reason to fear the gods of this world.

You have given your statutes, ordinances, law, and commandment that I might live. And yet I often stiffen at them. I know, however, it is your perfect love for me that will cast out all fear.

DAY 72

*II Kings 17:38 And the covenant that I have made with you ye shall not forget; **neither shall ye fear** other gods.*

Covenant is acted out in two ways: Remembrance and Lovingkindness. Covenant partners remember their promise to defend each other when threatened by an enemy. They act in lovingkindness even if it endangers their own life. God has never forsaken His covenant responsibilities. Remember this and fear not.

Oh, Father, how forgetful I am of your lovingkindness toward me. You have kept every covenant promise. I know you will continue to be faithful. I must ask myself today if I am fulfilling all of my covenant responsibilities toward you.

DAY 73

1Chronicles 16:30 Fear before Him, all the earth: the world also shall be stable, that it be not moved.

The Ark of the Covenant has finally been returned to Jerusalem, and David rejoices with a psalm. What God determines to stand firm shall stand firm until His sovereignty allows a change. Rejoice today in the stability of your Lord.

All the earth is yours, and I am only a steward of the things you have put in my charge. I know that nothing shall be added or taken away without your consent. Help me to be satisfied with all that you permit, even when I don't presently see its purpose.

DAY 74

Psalm 24:7-9 Lift up your heads, O ye gates; and be ye lift up, ye everlasting doors; and the King of glory shall come in. Who is this King of glory? The LORD strong and mighty, the LORD mighty in battle. Lift up your heads, O ye gates; even lift them up, ye everlasting doors; and the King of glory shall come in. Who is this King of glory? The LORD of hosts, he is the King of glory. Selah.

This was David's song for the return of the Ark of the Covenant to Jerusalem. What a reminder to us that when Christ is on the throne of our life, we can lift up our heads because He is strong and mighty in both the spiritual and physical realm.

I have a feeling that your church will one day sing this song at the end of the battle. However, as we wait for that day and you tabernacle within me, I desire to be a living example of David's exaltation.

DAY 75

*Psalm 92:1-3 It is a good thing to give thanks unto the LORD, and to sing praises unto thy name, O most High: To show forth thy **lovingkindness** in the morning, and thy faithfulness every night, upon an instrument of ten strings, and upon the psaltery; upon the harp with a solemn sound.*

It is often through music that our spirits are lifted and we are reminded of God's unfailing attributes. Remember that our praise should show forth His character, rather than showplace our talent.

May my praise be music to your ears, O Lord, and a fitting proclamation of your character.

DAY 76

*1 Chronicles 28:20 And David said to Solomon his son, "Be strong and of good courage, and do it: **fear not,** nor be dismayed: for the LORD God, even my God, will be with thee; He will not fail thee, nor forsake thee, until thou hast finished all the work for the service of the house of the LORD.*

David knew that his dream to build the temple would not be accomplished in his own time, so he helped Solomon build his dreams on the promises of their covenant God. As a wise father often does, he looked to the scripture and repeated the words Moses spoke in passing the torch to Joshua. It is imperative that we hold tight to God's truth ourselves while encouraging the younger generation with the promises we have found to be faithful.

Your faithfulness has never been in question. As I pass the torch to the next generation, I would have them see this in my life as well as hear it with my words.

DAY 77

*II Chronicles 20:15 And he said, "Hearken ye, all Judah, and ye inhabitants of Jerusalem, and thou king Jehoshaphat, Thus saith the LORD unto you, '**Be not afraid** nor dismayed by reason of this great multitude; for the battle is not yours, but God's.'"*

The Spirit of the LORD was speaking through Jahaziel in response to all of Judah, led by Jehoshaphat, seeking God by fasting and prayer. Have you met face to face with the commander-in-chief, or are you trying to fight battles in your own strength?

Oh, how often I try to fight my own battles when my deliverer is standing by, waiting for me to relinquish my personal objectives. It is not my battle. I am your servant. Help me to remember that time spent in fasting and prayer before the battle often negates the battle itself.

DAY 78

Ephesians 6:10 Finally, my brethren, be strong in the Lord, and in the power of his might.

Whether by David's words to Solomon, Moses words to Joshua, or Paul's words to the Ephesians, God continually speaks peace and strength through His servants to the next generation of leaders. We must hold fast to these admonitions by putting on the full armor ourselves and finding our strength in the power of His might. (See Appendix A)

Father, I know what happens when I fail to dress up in Jesus Christ. I have tried to fight the flaming missiles without a faith-soaked shield. I have walked into enemy territory without my belt of truth securing the rest of my armor in place, and the results were disastrous! Thank you for the defeats which have taught me to dress up in Jesus every day.

DAY 79

*II Chronicles 20:17 Ye shall not need to fight in the battle; set yourselves, stand ye still, and see the salvation of the LORD with you, O Judah and Jerusalem: **fear not**, nor be dismayed; tomorrow go out against them for the LORD will be with you.*

More often than not, this is the way the LORD chooses to take care of our enemies. While God's people sang His praises, the LORD set ambushes against the enemy and they were routed. The enemies of God's people actually destroyed one another. Can you bury your pride and let God defeat your enemies also?

Stepping out in self-confidence would be detrimental, but stepping out in God-confidence is victorious. How I long for this to be the rule of my life.

DAY 80

*II Chronicles 32:7 Be strong and courageous, **be not afraid** nor dismayed for the king of Assyria, nor for all the multitude that is with him: for there be more with us than with him.*

There is never a time when the enemy and his adversaries outnumber the army of our Lord. Revelation 5:11 speaks of myriads of myriads and thousands upon thousands of angels along with the living creatures and elders surrounding God's throne. A myriad can be 10,000 or an unidentifiable large number. And each one is ready to do God's bidding at all times.

It is easy to feel lonely in a crowd of people that I do not know, especially if the majority of them do not claim you as Lord. Thank you for this reminder that we who belong to the King of kings are never ever outnumbered.

DAY 81

*Psalm 103:1-4 Bless the LORD, O my soul: and all that is within me, bless his holy name. Bless the LORD, O my soul, and forget not all his benefits: Who forgiveth all thine iniquities; who healeth all thy diseases; Who redeemeth thy life from destruction; who crowneth thee with **lovingkindness** and tender mercies; Who satisfieth thy mouth with good things; so that thy youth is renewed like the eagle's.*

As we bow toward the Lord, we realize how impoverished we would be without His benefits—sinful, diseased, shattered, unloved, unsatisfied, and used up humans with no hope for improvement.

Oh, my El Shaddai, you truly are the All-Sufficient One. I am so needy and you are complete. May my life show forth your sufficiency rather than my deficit.

DAY 82

*Nehemiah 5:9 Also I said, "It is not good that ye do: ought ye not to walk in the **fear of our God** because of the reproach of the heathen our enemies?"*

The scrutiny of those who have not put their trust in our Lord is a powerful motive for seeking to glorify God in all we do. Do I listen to His Word? Do I honor and obey it? Could my disobedience hinder another from coming to a saving knowledge of our Lord Jesus Christ?

Show me any area of my life, Father, where I am not living above reproach and strengthen me to make the change.

DAY 83

*Psalm 143:8 Cause me to hear thy **lovingkindness** in the morning; for in thee do I trust: cause me to know the way wherein I should walk; for I lift up my soul unto thee.*

Can we hear God's lovingkindness? David expected God to speak to him in the morning and give him instructions for his day. He participated by giving ear to the Lord's teaching and trusting what he heard.

Father, I ask with David that you would cause me to know the way in which I should walk. I know that my part is to trust what you tell me even though it may not gain acceptance in this world. Thank you for the reminders of your lovingkindness in the early morning hours.

DAY 84

*Nehemiah 4:14 And I looked, and rose up, and said unto the nobles, and to the rulers, and to the rest of the people, **Be not ye afraid** of them: remember the Lord, which is great and terrible, and fight for your brethren, your sons, and your daughters, your wives, and your houses.*

There will always be opposition to God's work just as Nehemiah encountered with the rebuilding of Jerusalem's walls. But Nehemiah speaks to us even today with the reminder that our God is great and terrible, giving us both the strength and ability to fight while rebuilding the walls that the enemy has plundered in our lives. We do this not only for ourselves, but for those who come behind us and for our Lord.

Father, I want my life to be a witness to your faithfulness. Give me the strength to fight when it is necessary and allow me to be a living example of the work that can be accomplished through the power of our Mighty God.

DAY 85

*Nehemiah 5:15 But the former governors that had been before me were chargeable unto the people, and had taken of them bread and wine, beside forty shekels of silver; yea, even their servants bare rule over the people; but so did not I, because of the **fear of God.***

Nehemiah practiced godly leadership in that he did not exploit the people under his authority for personal gain as previous governors had done. Christ reminds us that we are to love one another so that all men will know that we are His disciples (John 13:35).

As I consider my relationships with those around me, make me aware of any ulterior motives that are not from a pure heart.

DAY 86
*Psalm 119:88 Quicken me after thy **lovingkindness**; so shall I keep the testimony of thy mouth.*

When the world has dug its pit and is waiting for us to fall in it and forsake the precepts of our Lord we can ask Him to revive us in His lovingkindness. When we are hurt, angry, brokenhearted, and feeling unloved, it is the Holy Spirit of God living within us who reminds us to *"Press toward the mark for the prize of the high calling of God in Christ Jesus."*

Here I am again Lord, in need of the great exchange, my weakness for your strength, my desire to lash out replaced with your lovingkindness. It is very difficult in my flesh, but I will open up my heart and allow you to fill it once again from the vast reservoir of your kindness and mercy. How grateful I am that you never tire of my asking! I love you Lord.

DAY 87

*Job 1:8 And the LORD said unto Satan, Hast thou considered my servant Job, that there is none like him in the earth, a perfect and an upright man, one that **feareth God**, and escheweth evil?*

Look at the words God used to describe Job. As God's servant, he was different than the rest of the world. He had a humble, obedient trust in the One he served and fled from the evil that His master warned against. How would God describe you? Does your fear of the Lord make you flee from evil, or do you dismiss God's wisdom and run headlong into the snare of the trapper?

Father, I know Job was not sinless, but he was sincere in his faith and humbly obedient to your Word. I pray that you would help me to live a life which could be described in similar terms.

DAY 88

*Job 9:34-35 Let him take his rod away from me, and let not his fear terrify me: Then would I speak, and not **fear him**; but it is not so with me.*

Job knows that the fear of the Lord is not meant to terrify us but to lead us to respect, even when we don't understand His ways. However, at this moment in his life he is only reminding himself of that truth. He is being honest by saying that his feelings are not reconciled with his intellect. Our feelings are so shallow and often betray the truth to us. Base your trust in God on facts not on feelings.

It all boils down to faith, doesn't it? The assurance of things hoped for, and the conviction of what I know to be true even if my eyes are not beholding it at the moment. That you love me and have my best interest at heart has never been in question.

DAY 89

*Job 28:28 And unto man he said, Behold, the **fear of the Lord**, that is wisdom; and to depart from evil is understanding.*

Job quotes what He has learned from the Almighty God. He speaks in this verse of true wisdom and real understanding, accepting no substitutes. They are impossible to grasp outside of reverencing and submitting to our Holy God.

Holy Father, I want this wisdom of which you speak and understanding to go with it. Show me the places in my life where I have been irreverent or unsubmissive. Help me to quickly identify evil and give me the strength and agility to run from it at all times.

DAY 90

*Job 31:34 Did I **fear** a great multitude, or did the contempt of families terrify me, that I kept silence, and went not out of the door?*

Job did not fear man because he had no sin to hide. He knew that sin hidden before God is exposed before man (II Samuel 12:12). Is there any fear in your life that has it's origination in guilt? If so take it straight to the Father so that the accuser of the brethren has no grounds on which to keep you bound.

Guilt is a terrible chain with which to bind myself. I repent of those past sins for which you have died, and I take your key of forgiveness to unlock those chains that have bound me for so long. Thank you for your sanctifying work which purchased my freedom! When I am free before you, I need not cower before man.

DAY 91

*Job 37:24 Men do therefore **fear him**; he respecteth not any that are wise of heart.*

God has His reasons for what He does. He has earned our respect many times over. We do not need to figure Him out or see the whole picture in order to trust Him.

Almighty God, you are exalted in power and perfect in judgment; awesome majesty surrounds you. Why would I ever want my own way when your knowledge is from everlasting to everlasting?

DAY 92

*Psalm 3:6 I will **not be afraid** of ten thousands of people, that have set themselves against me round about.*

Many people, possibly even our own family, will set themselves against us in this life if we choose to stand for God's righteousness. But we can say with David as he fled from his son, Absalom, that we will not be afraid, because salvation belongs to the LORD our God.

Help me never to be afraid of standing for your righteousness regardless of the opposition.

DAY 93

*Psalm 27:3 Though an host should encamp against me, my heart shall **not fear**: though war should rise against me, in this will I be confident.*

Has your enemy become an army of sorts? Is it often the suspense of what is to come that causes you to fear? David was able to hold up his shield of faith when thoughts of future battles attempted to shatter his present peace. Recall God's faithfulness and be confident in your head as well as your heart.

Some of the battles I worried about did come to pass, but never did I fight one of them alone. You have supplied everything needed to stand and face the enemy, and I've emerged much stronger from the experience.

DAY 94

*Psalm 34:7 The angel of the LORD encampeth round about them that **fear him**, and delivereth them.*

This is divine protection from the Most High God. There is not a bodyguard on this earth who could do a better job.

What an encouragement, LORD, that you set up camp around me and deliver me from anything that would not be for my eventual good. I realize that this is a conditional promise, being for those who fear you.

DAY 95

*Psalm 34:11-14 Come, ye children, hearken unto me: I will teach you the **fear of the LORD**. [12] What man is he that desireth life, and loveth many days, that he may see good? [13] Keep thy tongue from evil, and thy lips from speaking guile. [14] Depart from evil, and do good; seek peace, and pursue it. [15] The eyes of the LORD are upon the righteous, and his ears are open unto their cry.*

David could have instructed us in many things, but of utmost importance was the fear of the LORD. Notice that the fear of the LORD involves our total being. It is not just a state of mind (vv.13-14). Who are these instructions for? They are for the one who desires a good life and many days.

I do desire a good life, Father. I want as many days as you deem best. Consecrate my lips, my tongue and my whole being so that your eyes and ears are pleased with what is seen and heard of your adopted child.

DAY 96

*Psalm 46:1-3 God is our refuge and strength, a very present help in trouble. [2] Therefore **will not we fear**, though the earth be removed, and though the mountains be carried into the midst of the sea; [3] Though the waters thereof roar and be troubled, though the mountains shake with the swelling thereof. Selah*

When you are in a tight place and there seems to be no breathing room, God is there with you. If that on which you depend is no longer trustworthy, He is your refuge. When everything seems to crumble around you, the God of creation is a sure foundation. Before your strength fails, allow Him to be your strength.

The mountains have been quaking and the wind picks up our worldly treasures only to throw them down in shambles. Nevertheless, you are there; I have experienced your presence in the midst of the storm. I know there are more storms coming, but their fierceness is no match for your faithfulness.

DAY 97

Psalm 49:16, 17 **Be not thou afraid** *when one is made rich, when the glory of his house is increased; For when he dieth he shall carry nothing away: his glory shall not descend after him.*

We must be careful not to grow envious or anxious when ungodly men and women prosper in this life. We can be certain that it is only a temporary shelter for them. It is, however, our responsibility to tell them about the eternal shelter that is available through our Lord.

Help me, Lord, to set my affection on the things above and not on the things of the earth. Give me boldness to lovingly share your truth with others.

DAY 98

Psalm 56:3 What time I am afraid I will trust in Thee.

David was honest by saying that there were times when fear entered his being. He knew how to handle the fear though, rather than allowing the fear to handle him.

What a simple verse to recall to mind, and yet so great a truth. Etch it on my very soul, Lord.

DAY 99

*Psalm 56:4 In God I will praise His Word, in God I have put my trust; I will **not fear** what flesh can do unto me.*

Faith is the counterbalance of fear. Praise releases the firm grip with which fear would have us bound. What is flesh in the face of our transcendent God?

What is flesh in the face of my God? Merely dust. However, it is the dust upon which the enemy dines. As I become a living sacrifice, I choose not to make my flesh available to the serpent.

DAY 100

Psalm 56:11 In God have I put my trust: I will not be afraid what man can do unto me.

David's word for man in this verse is *Adam*. Putting our confidence in the One who created Adam should diminish our fear of the created.

Just as David had to constantly remind himself and others where his trust was anchored, I choose to do the same. You only, Lord, are worthy of my confidence.

DAY 101

*Psalm 69:16, 17 Hear me, O LORD; for thy **lovingkindness** is good: turn unto me according to the multitude of thy tender mercies. And hide not thy face from thy servant; for I am in trouble: hear me speedily.*

Although this Psalm was written by David when he was surrounded by his adversaries, it foreshadows Christ's suffering and gives us a specific prayer for those times when there is trouble on every side. Notice that David often reminds himself of God's lovingkindness when the evidence seems to say that God has forgotten him.

My Very Present Help in Times of Trouble, thank you for hearing my cry time and time again. I am in awe that you would allow me to be a partaker of the multitude of your tender mercies.

DAY 102

*Psalm 78:53 And he led them on safely, so that they **feared not**: but the sea overwhelmed their enemies.*

What caused God's chosen people to be free from fear at the Red Sea? His leadership. We may not see the pillar of fire or the cloud of His glory today, but God's Holy Spirit resides within His children guiding in much the same manner.

Lead me safely, LORD through the paths of your righteousness.
When I go through the waters, I know you will be with me and
they will not engulf me.

DAY 103

*Psalm 91:5 Thou shalt **not be afraid** for the terror by night;*
nor for the arrow that flieth by day.

Psalm 91 has often been entitled "The Hiding Place." Verses
5-10 remind us that evil is very real, but if we choose to dwell
in the shelter of the Most High we need not fear it.

You have never told me to deny that evil is all around. You
have given me a shelter in which to dwell so that I am not open
game for the one who seeks to break my confidence. Thank you
for covering me with your pinions and sheltering me under
your wings.

DAY 104

Psalm 111:10 The fear of the LORD is the beginning of wisdom:
a good understanding have all they that do his commandments:
his praise endureth for ever.

When we have a good understanding of a job description and
do it without hesitation, others can pattern our actions. It is a
wise manager who puts this laborer in charge. Do you have a
good understanding of God's calling upon your life? Do you
follow through with His commands? Can others easily and
joyfully follow your example? If so our Lord will be praised.

I desire to follow your commands because I understand your faithfulness. Help me to walk in such a way that others would be blessed if they follow the example I put before them.

DAY 105

*Psalm 112:7 He shall **not be afraid** of evil tidings: his heart is fixed, trusting in the LORD.*

Psalm 112 lists several blessings that come to those who fear the LORD. One of the many is that we do not fear the arrival of bad news. Why? Because our heart is fixed on God's faithfulness in all things. When we fix our gaze all other sights are filtered out. When we fix our heart, the enemy's dart of fear can pierce us no longer.

Father, you have given me ample reason to trust you in all things. When my heart and mind begin to wander, help me to once again fix my gaze upon you.

DAY 106

*Psalm 112:8 His heart is established, he shall **not be afraid**, until he see his desire upon his enemies.*

During Christ's time upon this earth in human form He encountered many enemies, but His heart was established and He was never afraid. Why? He knew that His father would be faithful to His word and His enemies would soon become His footstool. We too must trust what God has said about those who oppose the Jesus they see in us. They have been set in slippery places and their end is destruction (Psalm 73:18).

Lord, you told us that because many hated you they will also hate us. Help me to keep an eternal perspective and be a salty saint even when the pressure is great.

DAY 107

*Psalm 118:6 The LORD is on my side; I will **not fear**: what can man do unto me?*

The covenant keeping God is your advocate, always acting in lovingkindness towards you. There is no more suitable ally since the mightiest men are but dust compared to God.

My will or your will, I must make the choice. Your will is that I no longer fear what man can do to me, but replace that with a holy devotion to you. I choose your will. I realize that the choosing is not enough; I must follow through.

DAY 108

*Psalm 119:149 Hear my voice according unto thy **lovingkindness**: O LORD, quicken me according to thy judgment.*

The Psalmist saw the wicked drawing near, but he knew that the Lord was even nearer, inspecting the enemy's heart as well as his own. The Sovereign Lord doesn't miss a beat.

The fact that you would hear my voice according to your lovingkindness and not according to my merit baffles me, LORD. But I thank you that even though righteousness and justice are the foundation of your throne, you have given me the judgment of mercy day after day. Revive me according to your judgment since mine often fails.

DAY 109

*Prov. 1:7 The **fear of the LORD** is the beginning of knowledge: but fools despise wisdom and instruction.*

A healthy respect for His majesty only begins the process of what He has in store for you. "*Call unto me, and I will answer thee, and shew thee great and mighty things, which thou knowest not (Jeremiah 33:3).* The fool, on the other hand, is caught up in himself and creates his own demise.

I do not want to be a fool, Father. Show me those great and mighty things that I have yet to see and understand about you.

DAY 110

Matthew 7:24,26 Therefore whosoever heareth these sayings of mine, and doeth them, I will liken him unto a wise man, which built his house upon a rock…And every one that heareth these sayings of mine, and doeth them not, shall be likened unto a foolish man, which built his house upon the sand…

We see from this passage that wisdom is much more about the doing than about the knowing. What is the foundation of your life? Have you built your house upon The Rock or sinking sand?

I want to build my life upon your wise instruction, Jesus. In doing so, it eliminates the fear of future failure.

DAY 111

*Proverbs 1:29 For that they hated knowledge, and did not choose the **fear of the LORD**...*

Respect for the LORD our God is a choice on this side of eternity. *One day every knee will bow and every tongue will confess that Jesus Christ is LORD to the glory of God the Father (Philippians 2:10-11).* Ignorance will be no excuse at the time of final judgment: Romans 1 tells us that since the creation of the world God's invisible attributes, His eternal power, and His divine nature have been clearly seen and understood through what has been made so man is without excuse.

I make the choice today, Lord, to respect and honor you with my life. Show me any areas where I have been quenching your Spirit and not walking in the light you have given me.

DAY 112

*Proverbs 2:3-5 Yea, if thou criest after knowledge, and liftest up thy voice for understanding; If thou seekest her as silver, and searchest for her as for hid treasures; Then shalt thou understand the **fear of the LORD**, and find the knowledge of God.*

Notice the verbs in these verses: cry, lift, seek, search, understand, find. Wisdom does not just happen upon us because we are God's children. We must expend some energy to obtain wisdom. We will understand the fear of the LORD and find the knowledge of God when we are students of His ways.

Father, as I cry out after knowledge, and lift my voice for understanding I realize that much of what I'm asking for will come through life's experiences. Thank you for your gentleness as you instruct me in the ways of righteousness.

DAY 113
*Proverbs 3:7 Be not wise in thine own eyes: **fear the LORD**, and depart from evil.*

In man's own wisdom he has departed from the Lord and embraced evil. Our own eyes have such a tendency to deceive us. Wisdom is the ability to see all of life through God's point of view. Ask the Father to show you where your own knowledge has led you away from His wisdom. He will compassionately lead you back to His plan which is much better than your own.

Show me, Lord, where my knowledge has led me away from your wisdom. I know your plans are what I would choose for myself if I had the insight to do so.

DAY 114
*Proverbs 3:24 When thou liest down, thou shalt **not be afraid**: yea, thou shalt lie down, and thy sleep shall be sweet.*

This proverb is a benefit to those who heed the instruction of v. 21, which encourages us to keep sound wisdom and discretion.

Times of rest are necessary for our bodies to continue functioning, and being at peace with God is necessary in order to have true rest.

Father, I know that true wisdom is seeing any situation from your point of view. With this in mind I can lie down and sleep knowing that your eyes will never close and you are sovereignly controlling all that comes into and out of my life.

DAY 115

*Proverbs 3:25,26 **Be not afraid** of sudden fear, neither of the desolation of the wicked, when it cometh. For the LORD shall be thy confidence, and shall keep thy foot from being taken.*

How do I have peace of mind? *"Thou wilt keep him in perfect peace whose mind is stayed on Thee: because He trusteth in Thee" (Isaiah 26:3).* Both of these passages remind us where our confidence must lie if we are to be free from fear. All our confidence must rest on the LORD our God who never sleeps and never tires of protecting His precious children.

How grateful I am, Lord, that you promise to guard my heart and mind. I confess to you that sudden fear has often overtaken me and I'm concerned about the desolation of the wicked. I choose to believe this, your Word, instead of my fears.

DAY 116

*Proverbs 8:13 The **fear of the LORD** is to hate evil: pride, and arrogancy, and the evil way, and the froward mouth, do I hate.*

If God is love then we are to abhor what is the opposite; not only in others, but also in ourselves.

All of these sins mentioned have knocked on my heart's door at one time or another. Help me, LORD, to always recognize them for what they are and turn them away promptly.

DAY 117

Galatians 5:22, 23 But the fruit of the Spirit is love, joy, peace, longsuffering, gentleness, goodness, faith, meekness, temperance; against such there is no law.

If we are walking with the Lord we will not only hate what He hates, but we will also love what He loves. God loves people and desires that we respond to them in the way in which He responds to us. This fruit is the evidence of God's character in our lives.

The best fruit is produced from a tree that has been carefully pruned. I don't look forward to the process, but I desire the results of your loving hand upon this branch.

DAY 118

*Proverbs 19:23 The **fear of the LORD** tendeth to life: and he that hath it shall abide satisfied; he shall not be visited with evil.*

Proverbs are general principles for those who would guide their life by them. If you do not find your satisfaction in God, then you may be shopping for contentment in places where evil is lurking. Does evil ever approach those who fear the LORD? Yes, Jesus was a perfect example, but He opened the door of escape with the scriptures. Part of fearing the LORD is running from sin where evil lurks, seeking whom it may devour.

Thank you, Lord, for the satisfaction that accompanies my salvation. Give me eyes to see evil lurking around the corner and the strength to take the door of escape. As Paul admonished the saints in Rome, I desire to be wise in what is good and innocent in what is evil (Romans 16:19b).

DAY 119

*Proverbs 23:17 Let not thine heart envy sinners: but be thou in the **fear of the LORD** all the day long.*

If your heart envies sinners take the time to read Psalm 73. Asaph had to come to the sanctuary of God in order to get his vision realigned because of that same mind set. When he changed his focus to the Lord he realized that he had judged by the mere sight of the situation like an animal that has no ability to reason. We are not mere animals. We can set our mind on the things of God and be refreshed remembering that He is the strength of our heart and our portion forever.

You are the strength of my heart, Lord, and my portion forever.

DAY 120

Proverbs 24:21-22 My son, fear thou the LORD and the king; and meddle not with them that are given to change: For their calamity shall rise suddenly; and who knoweth the ruin of them both?

Fearing the Lord and honoring the king walk hand in hand since God establishes our rulers. (Romans 13:1) Because evil men seek rebellion, friendships with those who defy authority are destined for trouble. I have found prayer to be much more effective than rebellion when I disagree with someone in authority over me.

Give me discernment to recognize those that are given to change. I do not want to be caught up in their calamity. I release to you my difficulties with authority. Help me to voice your opinion and not my own since I am a citizen of heaven first and then where you have placed me in society.

DAY 121

*Proverbs 31:21 She is **not afraid** of the snow for her household: for all her household are clothed with scarlet.*

The virtuous woman is not afraid that her family will be cold in the winter because she has made ample preparation to clothe them well. Some fears are a result of negligence on our part. Don't be slothful in your God-given responsibilities and God will not be slothful in His provision.

Thank you, Jehovah Jireh, for being our provider. May I be a good steward of what you have given me to manage.

DAY 122

*Ecclesiastes 7:18 It is good that thou shouldest take hold of this; yea, also from this withdraw not thine hand: for he that **feareth God** shall come forth of them all.*

Solomon has been writing about both wickedness and righteousness. We sometimes view life as unfair because we don't see the big picture. But God's final judgment will rectify all those seemingly inequitable situations.

Father, when I am having a pity party about the unjustness of society, bring to my mind the privileges we have as heirs of your promises.

DAY 123

*Ecclesiastes 8:13 But it shall not be well with the wicked, neither shall he prolong his days, which are as a shadow; because he **feareth not** before God.*

Although our earthly judges may fail to carry out retribution for the wicked, those who refuse to acknowledge God can not escape His hand no matter how far they run or where they try to hide. No man can prolong his days when God has determined that his time on earth has ended.

It is reassuring to know that your justice is righteous, and your judgment is final.

DAY 124

*Isaiah 7:4 And say unto him, "Take heed and be quiet; **fear not**, neither be fainthearted for the two tails of these smoking firebrands, for the fierce anger of Rezin with Syria, and of the son of Remaliah."*

There are those who will come against you to terrorize you and make for themselves a breach in your walls, but the Lord GOD says, *"It shall not stand nor shall it come to pass" (Isaiah 7:7)*. Like firewood your enemies will soon be burned up and gone. Just as Christ prayed for Peter when Satan desired to sift him as wheat; our intercessor, the Lord Jesus Christ, sits at the right hand of the Father interceding on your behalf.

I have often encountered angry men and women, and the anger is filtering down to the younger generations. Being quiet is not my natural reaction, but it can become my normal reaction with your help. Thank you, Jesus, for that constant intercession as my high priest.

DAY 125

*Isaiah 8:13 Sanctify the LORD of hosts himself; and **let him be your fear**, and let him be your dread.*

To sanctify means to set aside for a holy purpose. Have you set aside the LORD of hosts as holy, or have you given that position to a substitute? We often allow what we fear to have a dominant place in our thought processes, but God requires that we surrender our heart, soul, and mind to Him. (Deuteronomy 6:5, Matthew 22:37, Mark 12:30) Anything outside of our LORD God that has the most prominent place in our thought processes is misplaced because that is God's place.

75

Father, I want you to have all of me—my heart, soul, mind, and strength. May there always be abundant evidence that you occupy the throne in my life.

DAY 126

*Isaiah 10:24-25 Therefore thus saith the Lord GOD of hosts, O my people that dwellest in Zion, **be not afraid** of the Assyrian: he shall smite thee with a rod, and shall lift up his staff against thee, after the manner of Egypt. For yet a very little while, and the indignation shall cease, and mine anger in their destruction.*

Yes, Assyria would bring much pain to the children of Israel because of their disobedience, but they had ample warning and opportunity to turn from their wicked ways and avoid this captivity. However, God says that after a little while His productive anger will cease, and He will destroy those who do harm to His precious family, removing the burden.

Some of the "fear not" promises in your Word require faith in the midst of discipline. I know that your ways are higher than our ways and I must trust at all times.

DAY 127

*Isaiah 12:2 Behold, God is my salvation; I will trust, and **not be afraid**: for the LORD JEHOVAH is my strength and my song; he also is become my salvation.*

If God is your salvation the rest of this verse should be a fact of life for you. If He can come out of heaven to die for you and be raised from the dead to prepare your eternal home, then he can surely be trusted with your anxieties.

When my strength fails Lord, you remind me that real strength comes from you. When I don't feel like singing, Father, you sing to me through your Psalms, and I cannot help but agree in my spirit. You have become my salvation over and over and over again. I look forward to eternity with such a faithful friend.

DAY 128

Ephesians 6:10, 11 Finally, my brethren, be strong in the Lord, and in the power of his might. Put on the whole armor of God that ye may be able to stand against the wiles of the devil.

Paul reminds his brothers and sisters in Christ that we stand strong when we stand in the Lord's strength. The devil certainly is sly and cunning, but the covering we gain at salvation will protect all those who are willing to take a position against his deceit. You will find this firm stance to be unattainable on your own, but well within God's capabilities.

Never have I been able to be strong in the power of my own might. However, I have been privileged to watch you work through me and many others as we yielded to your authority in our lives. How I rejoice, Lord, that you have put me on the winning team and given me all the protection that I need.

DAY 129

Isaiah 31:4 For thus hath the LORD spoken unto me, like as the lion and the young lion roaring on his prey, when a multitude *of shepherds is called forth against him, he will **not be afraid** of their voice, nor abase himself for the noise of them: so shall the LORD of hosts come down to fight for mount Zion, and for the hill thereof.*

This world is full of noisy ones who mock God with their words and actions. Their challenge is no threat to Him. He will prevail.

Lord, you are the Lion of the tribe of Judah, but you are also my personal defender. I know that the defense of this world cannot compare to your might and power. Help me to not be afraid of or humiliated by the world's noise.

DAY 130

*Isaiah 33:6 And wisdom and knowledge shall be the stability of thy times, and strength of salvation: the **fear of the LORD** is his treasure.*

We can search far and wide for help in difficult times. We can even purchase a certain amount of assistance. Even so, all of that is of no avail if we lack respect for the LORD our God. His purposes will be accomplished regardless of our efforts to buy our way out of trouble.

LORD, you are my strength, my wisdom, my knowledge, and my treasure. I know that your purposes for my life will be accomplished. I want to cooperate with you in this and not be an enemy to myself.

DAY 131

*Jeremiah 9:23-24 Thus saith the LORD, Let not the wise man glory in his wisdom, neither let the mighty man glory in his might, let not the rich man glory in his riches: but let him that glorieth glory in this, that he understandeth and knoweth me, that I am the LORD which exercise **lovingkindness**, judgment, and righteousness, in the earth: for in these things I delight, saith the LORD.*

God might see fit to make us wise, mighty, or rich, but we must realize that we have received none of this on our own. In fact, we can have all of these blessings and still be impoverished if we are ignorant of the LORD MOST HIGH.

You delight to exercise lovingkindness, judgment, and righteousness, and I am delighted to be the recipient. How often I have come close to stumbling as I look upon the riches, might and wisdom that the world has to offer. Then I come to your Word, and you so gently remind me that those things are distracting me. Forgive me, Father, for using the world's measure rather than considering your kingdom's account.

DAY 132

*Isaiah 35:4 Say to them that are of a fearful heart, Be strong, **fear not**: behold your God will come with vengeance, even God with a recompense he will come and save you.*

Our Father often pairs strength with the absence of fear. That is because fear weakens us. It encourages us to take vengeance in our own hands. But none of us has permission from a holy God to do what He reserves for Himself. Leave it up to Him and your *"scorched land will become a pool" (v.7)*.

There is a lot of scorched ground in my life because I listened to my fear instead of beholding your faithfulness. However, scorched land can become very productive in the right conditions. Make it so in my life, Lord.

DAY 133

*Isaiah 37:6, 7 And Isaiah said unto them, thus shall ye say unto your master, thus saith the LORD, **be not afraid** of the words that thou hast heard, wherewith the servants of the king of Assyria have blasphemed me. ⁷ Behold, I will send a blast upon him, and he shall hear a rumor, and return to his own land; and I will cause him to fall by the sword in his own land.*

The law of the harvest rang true in the Old Testament as well as the New and will be manifested even in our lives today. The king of Assyria tried to intimidate God's people by shouting words, and God used words to turn the tide. Our enemies will reap what they sow, but be on guard because we too will do some reaping.

Father, words do hurt, but I know that you hear every syllable spoken to me as well as those that proceed from my own mouth. Help me to deliver words of grace and to leave the recompense of harsh words up to you.

DAY 134

*Isaiah 40:9-11 O Zion, that bringest good tidings, get thee up into the high mountain; O Jerusalem, that bringest good tidings, lift up thy voice with strength; lift it up, **be not afraid**;*

say unto the cities of Judah, Behold your God! [10] Behold, the Lord GOD will come with strong hand, and his arm shall rule for him: behold, his reward is with him, and his work before him. [11] He shall feed his flock like a shepherd: he shall gather the lambs with his arm, and carry them in his bosom, and shall gently lead those that are with young.

Jerusalem was given a bright and shining light so that she could share it with the rest of the world who was groping in darkness. She used the light to look for needles in a haystack rather than to show the world the way to God. Jesus fulfilled this Old Testament picture of the one Jerusalem was to behold and proclaim as God. He is the good shepherd who gathers and feeds, carries and leads his precious flock. Are you afraid to proclaim the truth or even believe it for yourself?

Jesus, how wonderful is your Word! We see you in both the Old Testament and the New, fulfilling every prophecy. You are the King, the Servant, the Man, and God that Isaiah and Zechariah said we should behold. As your purposes are revealed in my life, give me the courage to follow your lead (Zechariah 6:12, 9:9; Isaiah 40:9, 42:1).

DAY 135

*Isaiah 41:10 **Fear thou not**; for I am with thee; be not dismayed; for I am thy God. I will strengthen thee; yea, I will help thee; yea, I will uphold thee with the right hand of my righteousness.*

Are you trembling? Are you weak? Are you walking on unsteady ground in any area of your life? Or are you just trying to walk through this life in your own strength? If so follow His instructions and trust His commitments. Our instructions are to fear not, while He commits to be with us, strengthen us, help us, and uphold us with His mighty right hand. I would rather walk in the power of His might than in my own limitations.

Father, help me to remember that it matters not who I am alone, but whose I am and who you are. Each of my "I am not's" is overshadowed by your "I Am".

DAY 136

*Isaiah 41:13 For the LORD thy God will hold thy right hand, saying unto thee, **Fear not**; I will help thee.*

Why do we take the hand of a young child when we are in a crowd or a place of potential danger? So they can rely on our ability to negotiate the territory. God wants to help you negotiate the twists and turns of life with His omniscience and omnipotence. Will you be that stubborn child who pulls free and exposes himself to danger, or will you allow Him to be your helper and guide? Think about His position if His right hand is holding your right hand. There is little room for separation.

If your right hand is able to grasp my right hand then you are directly in front of me and/or immediately behind me. How comforting to know that through the gift of the Holy Spirit, you also dwell within me!

DAY 137

*Isaiah 41:14 **Fear not**, thou worm Jacob, and ye men of Israel; I will help thee, saith the LORD, and thy redeemer, the Holy One of Israel.*

A worm is weak, defenseless, and trampled on by everyone. However, our Redeemer, the Holy One, has set us up to be seated with Him in heavenly places, to be trampled on by no one. Your position is your choice.

My Redeemer, I choose to be blessed with every spiritual blessing in heavenly places, to be holy and blameless before you, and live to the praise of your glory, as the apostle Paul spoke of in his letter to the Ephesians.

DAY 138

*Isaiah 43:1 But now thus saith the LORD that created thee, O Jacob, and He that formed thee, O Israel, **Fear not**: for I have redeemed thee, I have called thee by thy name; thou art mine.*

He created you, He formed you, He redeemed you, He called you by name. That is proof enough that you are His. Since all other things were also created by Him and for Him (Colossians 1:16) we can confidently say that there is no reason to fear.

I know that you are dedicated to taking care of your own. You have purchased me, and I am yours. Once again I must agree in my heart with what I know in my mind and stand firm on the truth of your promises.

DAY 139

*Isaiah 43:5 **Fear not**: for I am with thee: I will bring thy seed from the east, and gather thee from the west;*

The primary focus here was the return of Israel from Babylon; but on a more personal note, we can rest assured that there are no barriers, distance or otherwise, that can hinder God's plans.

I have seen evidence of this many times over as you bring people together from very distant places who have a common acquaintance etc. I know you have specific plans all arranged. I don't want to miss the blessings because of my fearful heart.

DAY 140

*Isaiah 44:2 Thus saith the LORD that made thee, and formed thee from the womb, which will help thee; **Fear not**, O Jacob, my servant; and thou, Jesurun, whom I have chosen.*

This promise has been repeated over and over in the book of Isaiah. Is there any doubt in your mind that God made you, formed you from the womb, and has helped you in the past? If He has brought you this far would it not be outside of His nature to turn His back on you today? Remember He is the same yesterday, today, and forever.

The fact that you have chosen any of us baffles me, Lord. But the fact that you have chosen one like me throws me for a loop. I am so needy. But I guess that is part of the reason you chose me, isn't it?

DAY 141

*Isaiah 44:8 **Fear ye not**, neither be afraid: have not I told thee from that time, and have declared it? Ye are even my witnesses. Is there a God beside me? Yea, there is no God; I know not any.*

Keep this thought in mind: No matter how many people believe that they are as God or can become as a god, there is only One. He has declared it. If there were to be another The Omniscient One would surely know. Our reverence belongs to Him only.

Yes, I am a witness to your faithfulness. You know all things, Lord. And if you know no other gods then there are none. It is when I permit other things to have first place in my life that I begin to feel overwhelmed. I desire to have only you on the throne of my life.

DAY 142

*Isaiah 51:7 Hearken unto me, ye that know righteousness, the people in whose heart is my law; **fear ye not** the reproach of men, neither be ye afraid of their revilings.*

Our Lord is referring to more than just intellectual knowledge in this passage. If we have become one with God's righteousness through His Son Jesus Christ and are listening to Him above the voices of the world we need not fear what men may say against us. Our reputation is in His hands.

I know you, Christ, therefore I know righteousness. How thankful I am that you know my heart, inside and out. Help me to not be afraid of what others are saying as long as I represent you well, and remain above reproach in all things.

DAY 143

*Psalm 48:9-10 We have thought of thy **lovingkindness**, O God, in the midst of thy temple. According to thy name, O God, so is thy praise unto the ends of the earth: thy right hand is full of righteousness.*

As you enter the sanctuary to worship, what is on your mind? And who receives the most praise out of your day-to-day living? Is it the One who holds you in His right hand of righteous or do other matters get in the way? Make it a point to prioritize your thought life this very day.

I realize that I need help with this, Father. "The spirit is willing, but the flesh is weak." Remind me when I slip back into worldly thinking.

DAY 144

*Isaiah 54:4 **Fear not**; for thou shalt not be ashamed: neither be thou confounded; for thou shalt not be put to shame; for thou shalt forget the shame of thy youth, and shalt not remember the reproach of thy widowhood any more.*

At one time we were estranged from God just as Israel was estranged from Him. But He purchased our pardon; He bore our shame and reproach. He now leads us toward our inheritance, and does not dwell on our past. It is up to us to follow His lead.

You have never brought up my past sins, and yet I allow them to surface quite often. Help me forget as you do—not with a faulty memory, but by refusing to hold the sin to my account.

DAY 145

*Isaiah 54:14 In righteousness shalt thou be established: thou shalt be far from oppression; for thou shalt **not fear**: and from terror; for it shall not come near thee.*

We have no righteousness of our own. We are established in His righteousness only. This passage characterizes the reign of our Messiah. It will happen in the future for Israel. It can happen in our personal lives this very day.

That is my desire, Lord, to be so established and confident in your righteousness that I never fear because I feel inferior. Help me to not accept oppression even from myself.

DAY 146

Ephesians 6:14 Stand therefore, having your loins girt about with truth, and having on the breastplate of righteousness;

How often do we check the fit of our armor? If your belt of truth has been loosened at all then your breastplate may not be covering all your vital organs. It is essential that we not allow our armor to shift in any direction. It could make for a very difficult battle.

It is the truth of your Word which holds the rest of my armor in place. As I check the fit of all you have supplied for my covering, show me any chinks I might have allowed in the armor.

DAY 147

Isaiah 57:11 And of whom hast thou been afraid or feared, that thou hast lied, and hast not remembered me, nor laid it to thy heart? Have not I held my peace even of old, and thou fearest me not?

Once again, the fear of man gets God's people in trouble. He will not give His honor to another and neither should we.

You have been more than gracious to me, Father; and I know that it hurts you deeply when I feel the need to be untruthful to save my own flesh. Forgive me for considering my own well being as more important than my relationship with you.

DAY 148
Psalm 119:133 Order my steps in thy word: and let not any iniquity have dominion over me.

I agree with the Apostle Paul as he reminded the Romans that: *"sin should not be master over you because you are not under law but under grace."* If I allow fear to have dominion over me then my steps are certainly not ordered according to God's Word.

I desire these verses to ring true in my life, and I make them my prayer today, Most Holy God.

DAY 149
*Jeremiah 1:8 **Be not afraid** of their faces: for I am with thee to deliver thee, saith the LORD.*

Jeremiah was a naturally timid and sensitive young man whom God appointed to deliver a message of judgment against his own people. But God did not send him out alone, and neither will He send you out in your own strength. If you focus on the face of your Savior you have no need to be afraid of the faces in the periphery.

How often, Lord, I have told you that I was unfit for the task you laid before me. Yet there was no release from the obligation. Thank you for using my fears to show me your strength.

DAY 150

*Jeremiah 2:19 Thine own wickedness shall correct thee, and thy backslidings shall reprove thee: know therefore and see that it is an evil thing and bitter, that thou hast forsaken the LORD thy God, and that **my fear is not in thee**, saith the Lord GOD of hosts.*

Sometimes it is the dread of discipline that acts as a barrier to disobedience. When we forsake the LORD our God trying to forge our own paths and make our own alliances, our own sin will eventually correct us. Don't get angry with God. Any parent knows that natural consequences are the most effective discipline.

Many times you have warned me of the bitterness of my rebellion. Often I have had to taste those consequences. It has been the lust of the flesh, the lust of the eyes, and the woeful pride of life that I am prone to. I want the fear of the Lord to eclipse those desires in my heart.

DAY 151

*Jeremiah 5:22 Fear **ye not me?** Saith the LORD: will ye not tremble at my presence, which have placed the sand for the bound of the sea by a perpetual decree, that it cannot pass it:*

and though the waves thereof toss themselves, yet can they not prevail; though they roar, yet can they not pass over it?

What a reminder that our God is in control. If He set the borders of the mighty sea for our protection do we dare try to cross the personal boundaries He has set for us? To fear the Lord is to respect His authority knowing that He has lovingkindness as His motive.

You alone are holy, complete and perfect. Your persistence in my life is much more than I deserve. Thank you for the protective barriers you have built in my life. Forgive me for my outbursts when I see only the boundary and not the love behind it.

DAY 152

*Jeremiah 6:25 Go not forth into the field, nor walk by the way; for the sword of the enemy and **fear** is on every side.*

God has set a boundary with His written Word in your life. Don't transgress or "side-step" His protective barrier. The enemy is just beyond, waiting to gain control of your life through fear and manipulation.

Those boundaries that I've been trying to climb over and sneak around...I thank you for them. I know that by staying in your Word I'll recognize the borders that have been erected by you and also discover where the enemy's traps have been set.

DAY 153

*Jeremiah 10:5 They are upright as the palm tree, but speak not: they must needs be borne, because they cannot go. **Be***

not afraid *of them; for they cannot do evil, neither also is it in them to do good.*

God explains through the prophet Jeremiah how foolish it is to worship idols. They are mere pieces of wood decorated with silver and gold that have been fashioned by the hands of those who fear them. We too make idols in our own lives and then let them control us. Foolishness isn't it?

Those idols I have erected have had such a hold on me. Possessions, career, reputation, and even those who try to take them away often get more attention than I have given you. All I have has been given to me by you. Why would I worship such things? Forgive me, Lord.

DAY 154
Isaiah 26:3 Thou wilt keep him in perfect peace, whose mind is stayed on thee: because he trusteth in thee.

We must deliberately avoid destructive thought processes if we are to remain free from fear. How do we do so? By keeping our mind occupied with our Prince of Peace. This does take some practice, but the Holy Spirit is more than willing to give you a little nudge when your mind starts drifting.

Spirit of the Living God, would you please give me that gentle reminder when my mind begins to drift away from my Prince of Peace. Hold me accountable even in my thought life.

DAY 155
II Corinthians 10:3-5 For though we walk in the flesh, we do not war after the flesh: (For the weapons of our warfare are

not carnal, but mighty through God to the pulling down of strongholds;) Casting down imaginations, and every high thing that exalteth itself against the knowledge of God, and bringing into captivity every thought to the obedience of Christ…

Are you bringing every single thought into captivity? Is Christ welcome in all the rooms of your mind, or are there some doors that you would rather He not open? Victory awaits those who allow these truths take a firm hold in their lives.

Holy Spirit, show me those areas in my life where I have allowed even the smallest concern to exalt itself against the knowledge of my loving Father. Right now I name all that I am aware of that must be brought into captivity to the obedience of Christ. There is no need for me to dwell on them any longer. Set me free and help me to stay free!

DAY 156

*Jeremiah 10:7 Who would **not fear** thee, O King of nations? For to thee doth it appertain; forasmuch as among all the wise men of the nations, and in all their kingdoms, there is none like unto thee.*

The fear of the LORD is unlike what an earthly king would desire. Our relationship with the LORD is based on mutual respect and lovingkindness. Remember that He is the King of kings and LORD of lords. All will answer to Him and eventually bow the knee.

Teach me to have a healthy respect for authority knowing that all authority has been granted by you. However, I want none other than King Jesus to occupy the throne of my life.

DAY 157

Jeremiah 30:5 For thus saith the LORD; We have heard a voice of trembling, of fear, and not of peace.

This chapter begins the prediction of future restoration. It is not happening at the time of the writing but it will come to pass. God will hear the trembling and fearful voice of His people, even when they have been walking in disobedience.

You are looking ahead always to the time of restoration. It is my desire to remain obedient so that there will be no voice of trembling or fear because of rebelliousness on my part.

DAY 158

*Jeremiah 30:10 Therefore **fear** thou **not**, O my servant Jacob, saith the LORD; neither be dismayed, O Israel: for, lo, I will save thee from afar, and thy seed from the land of their captivity; and Jacob shall return, and shall be in rest, and be quiet, and none shall make him afraid.*

What will happen when God hears the cry of His children? He will answer with a promise of restoration. He can rescue you no matter how far you have strayed or where your land of captivity is located. Although He is merciful, we can expect to face some consequences for our disobedience.

Many times, Lord, you have saved me from afar when sin has held me captive. I desire to be free from those sins that have held me and walk in complete obedience so that none will make me afraid.

DAY 159

Jeremiah 32:39 And I will give them one heart, and one way, that they may fear me for ever, for the good of them, and of their children after them:

God's chosen people had been taken into captivity because of their divided heart. They had gone the way of the world, and the Father used the world to teach them a lesson. His plan as always was redemption. When He calls us to fear Him and walk in His ways it is for our good and the good of our children. He sees the traps that are not yet visible to us.

Father, it is both your desire and mine that I have an undivided heart. Thank you for giving me "one way" and for making that way clear in your written Word.

DAY 160

Jeremiah 31:3 The LORD hath appeared of old unto me, saying, Yea, I have loved thee with an everlasting love: therefore with **lovingkindness** *have I drawn thee.*

What a demonstration of God's lovingkindness! He knew us before we were born, with all of our inadequacies, sin, and selfishness; and yet he has been drawing us to Himself for a lifetime. Think back over your life and consider what God has used to draw you to Himself. The circumstances were not all joyful at the time, but they were intended to turn you towards the only one who can offer true joy and life everlasting.

My Lord and my God, it is often through difficult circumstances that you get our attention. You have not only been my life preserver, you have become my life. As with the apostle Paul, I exult in my tribulations, knowing that they bring perseverance, proven character, and hope.

DAY 161

*Jeremiah 32:40 And I will make an everlasting covenant with them, that I will not turn away from them, to do them good; but I will put **my fear** in their hearts, that they shall not depart from me.*

This is a verse of restoration. God is speaking here of the New Covenant through the Lord Jesus Christ. Because it is based on His righteousness and not our own, it is everlasting. Why did He say that He would put His fear in their hearts? That they should not depart from Him. Do you see the love in this action? He is constantly turned toward us to do us good. But where is your face more often turned? Toward Him or toward the world? The answer to that question may explain your propensity to fear.

Father, we are so prone to turn from our source of strength, provision, and peace. I know that I cannot change my own heart; it can only be done by the maker of the heart. Thank you for the cardiac surgery that is provided with the New Covenant.

DAY 162

Jeremiah 36:23, 24 And it came to pass, that when Jehudi had read three or four leaves, he cut it with the penknife, and cast it into the fire that was on the hearth, until all the roll was consumed in the fire that was on the hearth. ²⁴ Yet they were not afraid, nor rent their garments, neither the king, nor any of his servants that heard all these words.

There is a time to fear. It is when you have turned a deaf ear to or shown contempt for the Word of God. God will not turn a deaf ear to your defiance.

Father, keep me ever sensitive to your written, spoken, and living Word. I know that when my heart is hardened against what you have spoken, it is like casting your Word into the fire, and I am as guilty as Jehudi.

DAY 163

*Jeremiah 42:11 **Be not afraid** of the king of Babylon, of whom ye are afraid; be not afraid of him, saith the LORD: for I am with you to save you, and to deliver you from his hand.*

This admonition was to the few Jews who remained in the land of Judah after the deportation to Babylon. They were afraid of Babylonian retribution because the one appointed to govern them had been assassinated. God promised to protect them if they would stay and not flee to Egypt, but they were short on trust. Refusing to believe, they fled to Egypt and met their destruction.

My obedience indicates the value I place on your Word. May it prove to be more precious than gold in my life.

DAY 164

*Jeremiah 46:27 But **fear not** thou, O my servant Jacob, and be not dismayed, O Israel; for, behold, I will save thee from afar off, and thy seed from the land of their captivity; and Jacob shall return, and be in rest and at ease, and none shall make him afraid.*

Once again God reassures His people as He did before their captivity that He has plans to deliver them from the hand of the enemy and they will eventually experience rest and peace.

Fear and dismay, they sneak up on me so quickly and threaten my peace. I confess both to you, Father, realizing that you want them erased from my life.

DAY 165

*Jeremiah 46:28 **Fear** thou **not**, O Jacob my servant, saith the LORD: for I am with thee; for I will make a full end of all the nations whither I have driven thee: but I will not make a full end of thee, but correct thee in measure; yet will I not leave thee wholly unpunished.*

God will rescue us from the land of our captivity, but correction is coming. It will not be as harsh as the punishment that awaits the unbelievers who oppose Him, because we receive the mercy of a loving father along with our discipline. It will be no more than we deserve, or can bear, but sufficient to get the point across.

I need to be reminded, Lord, that just because I am being disciplined does not mean that you have left me. I realize that you cannot leave me without discipline, nor will you ever leave me in discipline. Thank you for your constant companionship especially when no human would want to put up with me.

DAY 166

*Lamentations 3:57 Thou drewest near in the day that I called upon thee; thou saidst, **Fear not**.*

The prophet Jeremiah uttered these lamentations as he sat on the hillside overlooking his desolate homeland. He had spoken all the words that the Lord had commanded him to speak, and Jerusalem would not listen. They even threw him into an empty cistern and left him to die in the mire. But God drew near and rescued him repeating His very familiar "Fear not" to his downtrodden servant.

Oh, Lord, I have never been thrown into a physical cistern, but I have been there emotionally. Thank you for not leaving me there to drown in the mire of my own self pity. I realize that it is my responsibility to obediently share your Word. The results are up to you.

DAY 167

*Ezekiel 2:6, 7 And thou, son of man, **be not afraid** of them, **neither be afraid** of their words, though briers and thorns be with thee, and thou dost dwell among scorpions: **be not afraid** of their words, nor be dismayed at their looks, though they be a rebellious house. ⁷ And thou shalt speak my words unto them, whether they will hear, or whether they will forbear: for they are most rebellious.*

Sometimes our Lord puts us in a "sticky" situation and asks us to accomplish a most difficult task. God knows the turmoil, for He instructed Ezekiel three times to not be afraid. If you have been given a similar assignment, focus on your instructor, not on your flesh, and hear the Father, Son, and Spirit saying, "Be not afraid."

Father, when the warfare is raging, and you put me on the front line with explicit instructions, give me the courage to go forth in your wisdom and strength, recognizing that obedience is my responsibility while the response of others is not.

98

DAY 168

Ezekiel 3:9 As an adamant harder than flint have I made thy forehead: fear not, neither be dismayed at their looks, though they be a rebellious house.

God has commanded us to speak and live truth before those who are so stubborn and obstinate that it seems we will never reach them. But guess what? He can make you even more steadfast than they. Don't give up or allow fear to overtake you. Obedience is your responsibility; softening their heart and mind is His.

Father, you told Ezekiel that if he did not warn the wicked man to turn from his ways and the wicked died in his iniquity, you would require his blood at Ezekiel's hand. Thank you for reminding me that the fear of the Lord is to be a greater force in my life than the fear of man.

DAY 169

*Daniel 10:12 Then said he unto me, **Fear not**, Daniel: for from the first day that thou didst set thine heart to understand, and to chasten thyself before thy God, thy words were heard, and I am come for thy words.*

Looking at Daniel's life we can see that prayer was never the last thing on his list. It was a priority with persistence. He had been fasting and praying for three weeks when this angel called Daniel by name speaking the now familiar, "fear not". Notice three things about Daniel's prayer: His priority – to understand, his position – humility, and the power – God responding with all the necessary resources.

So often, Lord, you have prepared answers to my prayers years ahead of time so that when my priorities and position were correct I was able to see your mighty power. Thank you for never being too late or too early, but always right on time.

DAY 170

*Daniel 10:19 And said, O man greatly beloved, **fear not**: peace be unto thee, be strong, yea, be strong. And when he had spoken unto me, I was strengthened, and said, Let my lord speak; for thou hast strengthened me.*

God quiets us with His peace and strengthens us with His Word. I have never heard the audible voice of God, but when He speaks to me with His written Word it is mighty powerful.

You give strength to the weary and to him who lacks might you increase power (Isaiah 40:29). The strength and peace that comes with your Word is no less than miraculous. Thank you for the spoken Word, the written Word, and the Living Word – my Lord Jesus Christ.

DAY 171

*Jeremiah 32:17,18 Ah Lord God! Behold, thou hast made the heaven and the earth by thy great power and stretched out arm and there is nothing too hard for thee: Thou shewest **lovingkindness** unto thousands, and recompensest the iniquity of the fathers into the bosom of their children after them: the Great, the Mighty God, the LORD of hosts, is his name.*

Think about the majesty and might of a Creator who could make the vast universe in only 6 days. Is it too difficult for Him to manage the troubles that you might encounter today? Not in the least. It is imperative, however, that we keep in mind the law of the harvest. God has always run the universe according to this law so that whatever we plant, that we will also reap. If we plant iniquity, iniquity will spring up even where we did not intend for it to. On the other hand, God's lovingkindness can be seen in generation after generation when one heart is given completely to Him.

Ah Lord God! You are the Mighty One. Whatever you decree will surely stand. Even though you are a God of mercy, I know that you are a just judge who allows us to suffer the consequences of sin just as your servant David suffered greatly because of his sin. How thankful I am that it did not render him useless in your kingdom. Make me a usable vessel for you.

DAY 172
*Joel 2:21 **Fear not**, O land; be glad and rejoice: for the LORD will do great things.*

In Joel's day the land had been stripped of its produce by invading locusts. Although God permits harsh things to occur in order to get our attention, He does not delight in our pain. As we "*rend our hearts and not just our garments*" (Joel 2:13) we experience His grace and compassion.

Lord God, I know that it is not the external change you most desire; although, it is evidence of what you have done internally. We will have reason to rejoice personally and nationally when we are obedient to you on the inside as well as the outside. Begin with me!

DAY 173

*Joel 2:22 **Be not afraid**, ye beasts of the field: for the pastures of the wilderness do spring, for the tree beareth her fruit, the fig tree and the vine do yield their strength.*

God's reproof not only affects people but also the land and the animals. Will He restore what the locusts have eaten? If we come to Him in repentance seeking reconciliation, He will most gladly restore and bless His children along with the beasts of the field and the land in which they dwell.

When I refuse to admit my sin I leave myself open for devastation and decay. Thank you, Lord, for the promise of reconciliation and renewal upon repentance.

DAY 174

*Amos 3:8 The lion hath roared, **who will not fear**? The Lord GOD hath spoken, who can but prophesy?*

If you are close enough to hear a lion's roar it is impossible to ignore. It is all the more true of the Lion of the Tribe of Judah. No one can claim ignorance of the works of the Lord GOD. They are as evident as the roar of a lion.

Father, we have heard you roar in our own nation and yet men and women go on as if they have not heard. You have always given ample warning before judgment, and I trust the truth of your Word concerning our national and personal waywardness. Open my ears to hear you clearly and circumcise my heart to obey you readily.

DAY 175

*Zephaniah 3:7 I said, Surely **thou wilt fear me**, thou wilt receive instruction; so their dwelling should not be cut off, howsoever I punished them: but they rose early, and corrupted all their doings.*

Children so often run the way of self-will regardless of known consequences. Suddenly the parent gets a glimpse of how God must feel when we deliberately disobey His explicit instructions, knowing full well the guaranteed results of our stubbornness.

I have been there, Father, deliberately going my own way knowing that the long term consequences of my actions will be very difficult to endure. And yet you continue to love me as a dedicated parent desiring to see a wayward child finally see the truth. Thank you for your persistence.

DAY 176

*Zephaniah 3:13 The remnant of Israel shall not do iniquity, nor speak lies; neither shall a deceitful tongue be found in their mouth: for they shall feed and lie down, and **none shall make them afraid.***

This prophecy is yet future for Israel and others who call upon the name of the Lord. It is only by the grace of our Good Shepherd that any of us will lie down in green pastures and be free from illegitimate fear.

Lord, I understand that fear came into the land along with sin. In that day when all sin is removed the same will be said of fear: no more to be found among us. Until that day help me to readily recognize any sin in my life and avert fear before it knocks on my door.

DAY 177

*Zephaniah 3:16 In that day it shall be said to Jerusalem, **Fear** thou **not**: and to Zion, Let not thine hands be slack.*

During the time of restoration Jerusalem is reminded to be diligent in obedience. Diligence to obey would also eliminate many fears in our own life today, would it not?

There is a time for me to rest and a time for me to be about your business. My spirit will rest in you, Lord, when I am careful to not let the relaxing interfere with the working.

DAY 178

*Haggai 2:5 According to the word that I covenanted with you when ye came out of Egypt, so my spirit remaineth among you: **fear** ye **not**.*

God has also given us the promise that His spirit will remain with us when we choose to come out of our Egypt (the world) and set our hearts toward the Promised Land (the abundant life). This should dispel many of our fears.

The promise that your Spirit would remain with me is such a comfort in this world of treachery where promises are thrown out the window and shattered like useless utensils. Thank you, Lord, for never making a hollow covenant, and for upholding them regardless of the difficulty.

DAY 179

*Zechariah 8:13 And it shall come to pass, that as ye were a curse among the heathen, O house of Judah, and house of Israel; so will I save you, and ye shall be a blessing: **fear not**, but let your hands be strong.*

This promise of future blessing was for those who would devote themselves to the rebuilding of the temple. They had been disciplined for their disobedience and will now be blessed for their return to God's work. It is the unknown that most often causes us to fear, but there is no reason to fear when God lays out His plan before us. We can be as sure of the blessing as we were of the discipline.

Holy God, may my hands be strengthened by you to do all that you have set before me. I desire to be a blessing to those around me, but more than that I desire to be a blessing to you.

DAY 180

Malachi 3:5 And I will come near to you to judgment; and I will be a swift witness against the sorcerers, and against the adulterers, and against false swearers, and against those that oppress the hireling in his wages, the widow, and the fatherless, and that turn aside the stranger from his right, and fear not me, saith the LORD of hosts.

Can you find yourself in the words of this judgment? God says that those who are involved in these things do not fear Him. He will be a swift witness and judge against each one. There will be no time for bargaining at that point. He does say in the following verses that if we return to Him, He will return to us.

Oh LORD of Hosts, there have been times when I could have shown a kindness to the widow, the fatherless, and the stranger; and yet I was distracted by the things I deemed more important. Forgive me, LORD. I have the desire to turn from my agenda to yours, ever watchful for your leading in these areas.

DAY 181

*Matthew 1:20 But while he thought on these things, behold, the angel of the Lord appeared unto him in a dream, saying, Joseph, thou son of David, **fear not** to take unto thee Mary thy wife: for that which is conceived in her is of the Holy Ghost.*

This is the first "fear not" in the New Testament. The New Covenant would bring about major changes in the lives of those who believed in God. Would they take to heart the message given to Joseph—that the Holy Spirit would operate in a way they never thought possible, that God could actually come to earth clothed in a human tabernacle, that there was no longer a need for a priest to mediate between God and man? Joseph believed, as did many others, but still there were some who feared change and refused the truth. What about you? Is the truth difficult for you to accept? Will you let fear keep you from God's greatest blessings, or will you trust God's "fear not" even today?

Father, many of the things in your written Word are hard for me to accept. Even though it was difficult for Joseph to understand, he trusted you and was not disappointed. I want to be named among those who trust you whole-heartedly.

DAY 182

*Matthew 10:26 **Fear them not** therefore: for there is nothing covered, that shall not be revealed; and hid, that shall not be known.*

Jesus was speaking to His disciples as He sent them out as sheep among wolves. The religious leaders would do everything in their power to hide the truth just as many political leaders do today. But what encouragement we have that all truth will eventually be made known. So fear not those in authority who hide the truth and speak evil of you. God is still on the throne and Truth shall reign once again.

Father, I bring before you all of those in leadership who hide the truth in order to promote their agendas. Help me keep my focus on you, ensuring that the things to be revealed in my own life give honor to my King.

DAY 183

*Matthew 10:28 And **fear not** them which kill the body, but are not able to kill the soul: but rather fear him which is able to destroy both soul and body in hell.*

A man can kill my physical body and my soul will be separated from it; however, there is nothing a man can do to separate my soul from God since I have given it to Him.

By giving up I have gained, by letting go I have received. Thank you for being the keeper of my soul.

DAY 184

Matthew 10:31 **Fear ye not** *therefore, ye are of more value than many sparrows.*

A sparrow falling to the ground may seem insignificant to us, but it does not happen outside of the Father's knowledge since everything He created has value and a purpose. We were created in His image, made in His likeness. God desires that His namesake give a correct estimate of Him at all times. Nothing we do is insignificant to Him and it should not be to us.

Forgive me, Father, for the things I have done contrary to your image. Empower me to act in a way that glorifies you, even in the tasks which seem menial.

DAY 185

Matthew 14:26, 27 And when the disciples saw him walking on the sea, they were troubled, saying, It is a spirit; and they cried out for fear. [27] But straightway Jesus spake unto them, saying, Be of good cheer; it is I; **be not afraid**.

Our Lord often prepares the classroom for a memorable lesson by bringing along that which makes us extremely uncomfortable. Learning to focus on His power instead of our weakness is our first assignment.

How often my fears have given me false information, compelling me to focus on something other than your promises. I no longer want to be found in the classroom unprepared for your instructions. I'll need your gentle reminders of this passage.

DAY 186

*Matthew 17:6, 7 And when the disciples heard it, they fell on their face, and were sore afraid. ⁷ And Jesus came and touched them, and said, arise, and **be not afraid**.*

After seeing Jesus transfigured before them, and hearing the voice of God, Peter, James and John reacted just as any one else who has ever been in the presence of the Almighty. And what did Jesus do? He *touched them* not only with his hand, but with tenderness and compassion. A "fear not" from our Lord should cause us also to rise up from all forms of anxiety.

Would you, Lord, touch others through me as I share your faithfulness? Would you cause them to rise up from the burdens that have left them downtrodden and oppressed? Use me to show forth your glory and encourage others to be not afraid.

DAY 187

*Matthew 28:4, 5 And for fear of him the keepers did shake, and became as dead men. And the angel answered and said unto the women, **Fear not ye**: for I know that ye seek Jesus, which was crucified.*

Notice that the angel did not give the "fear not" admonition to the guards. They became as dead men. But to God's very own He sends a powerful message down through the ages… "Fear not you who name Jesus as Lord!" The tomb is empty and the victory has been won!

Risen Lord, I am in awe of your power, your majesty, and your personal touch on my life. Thank you for this message. I am thankful that the empty tomb means victory for me today as well as eternally.

DAY 188

*Matthew 28:8 And they departed quickly from the sepulchre with **fear** and great joy; and did run to bring his disciples word.*

These women were overwhelmed with emotion, experiencing both fear and great joy at the same time. They were fearful because of the unknown, but joyous because Jesus had risen just as He had said. These "mixed emotions" were channeled in a positive direction. They did not sit still, but followed the angel's instructions to go tell the disciples.

Lord, when I am experiencing mixed emotions help me to wisely sort through them in a positive and productive way, being careful to follow your instructions without hesitation.

DAY 189

*Matthew 28:10 Then said Jesus unto them, **be not afraid**: go tell my brethren that they go into Galilee, and there shall they see me.*

Jesus gave these women a message worth repeating: Be not afraid; Go tell; They shall see me. This same message, which began in the mouth of Christ, has been repeated down through the ages.

Father, use me to pass on that wonderful message that you first gave to women. May the excitement about your resurrection not fade with me but be ever increasing with passion as I continue to tell others that they will see you face to face.

DAY 190

*Mark 5:35, 36 While he yet spake, there came from the ruler of the synagogue's house certain which said, Thy daughter is dead: why troublest thou the Master any further? ³⁶ As soon as Jesus heard the word that was spoken, he saith unto the ruler of the synagogue, **Be not afraid**, only believe.*

Death puts us all on a level playing field doesn't it? Whether we be ruler or servant, we will all have to say farewell to someone we love and go through the grieving process. But praise be to our Lord Jesus Christ who has conquered death and the grave. He says to all who trust in his atoning work, "Be not afraid, only believe."

You, Lord, have taken the sting out of death. Our grieving, as Paul said, is not as those who have no hope. You are our hope, our assurance, that just as you died and rose again, the dead in Christ will also rise. You have provided for literally all of our human vulnerabilities. How could I do less than to give you my life?

DAY 191

*Mark 9:6, 7 For he wist not what to say; for they were sore **afraid**. ⁷ and there was a cloud that overshadowed them: and a voice came out of the cloud, saying, this is my beloved Son: hear him.*

Why do we fear that dreaded silence? So often we fill the air with nonsense when our Lord is trying to speak to someone. Let's learn from Peter's mistakes, knowing when to keep our mouth shut and our ears open.

I can only plead guilty when I read this passage. How often I have failed to hear you and have probably kept others from hearing you because of my needless conversation. Forgive me, Lord.

DAY 192

*Luke 1:13 But the angel said unto him, **Fear not**, Zacharias: for thy prayer is heard; and thy wife Elisabeth shall bear thee a son, and thou shalt call his name John.*

Here is a man whom the Bible describes as "*righteous before God, walking in all the commandments and ordinances of the Lord blameless*", and yet he was gripped with fear at the appearance of the angel of the Lord. Why? Because sinful man cannot bear the presence of one so pure. What was the angel's message? "*Thy prayer is heard.*" This most likely refers to a past prayer for a child and a present prayer for Israel. God wants us to know that He hears our prayers. He delights in answering them, often blessing many others through the desires of our hearts.

Lord, there is no way I can be blameless without your imputed righteousness, and still you have said, "So be it" to the desires of my heart. May your Holy Spirit always inspire my prayers in such a way that many are blessed by your answers.

DAY 193

*Luke 1:30 And the angel said unto her, **Fear not**, Mary: for thou has found favor with God.*

The Greek word for *favor* here is "charis" which is often translated *grace*. Mary was told not to fear what was happening in her life because she was a recipient of God's favor or grace. There are many things God has planned for your life which at the onset can cause you to be fearful, but let me remind you that "*of His fullness we have all received, and grace upon grace" (John 1:16).*

Father, it took a special kind of grace for a very special woman to accept the blessing you put upon Mary. I thank you that you also have specific tasks planned for me along with a promise that I too will receive the grace needed to follow through.

DAY 194

*Luke 2:10 And the angel said unto them, **Fear not**: for, behold, I bring you good tidings of great joy, which shall be to all people.*

Since the beginning of time, and especially since the birth of our Savior, our God has been able to turn our fears into great joy. When God is involved, the news is good news. His desire is for all people to have a future and a hope.

This is one of the most memorable "fear not" passages in all of scripture, and you have changed many lives with the same message that you sent to the shepherds that night. This good news has been the greatest joy in my life; how very grateful I am that you sent a Savior to all people, not just a select few.

DAY 195

Luke 5:9, 10 For he was astonished, and all that were with him, at the draught of the fishes which they had taken: and so *was also James, and John, the sons of Zebedee, which were partners with Simon. And Jesus said unto Simon, **Fear not**, from henceforth thou shalt catch men.*

Peter was so amazed at what had just taken place that Jesus spoke His peaceful "fear not". He would need to keep that in mind as Jesus explained that Peter and his fishing buddies were about to make a major career change. From now on their nets would bring in men rather than fish, and they would be supplying spiritual rather than physical food to the communities they entered.

Lord, sometimes I get so caught up in the physical that spiritual truth goes right over my head. Help me to see the spiritual lessons that you are teaching in the physical realm and accept the changes that you initiate in my life with faith instead of fear.

DAY 196

*Luke 8:50 But when Jesus heard it, he answered him, saying, **Fear not**: believe only, and she shall be made whole.*

According to Jesus, what should replace our fear even when a loved one must leave this earth? Faith is the answer, "only believe." Believe that what Jesus said is true. Believe that we do not weep as those who have no hope. Even as Jesus raised this young girl in front of her parents, He will one day bring with Him all those who have fallen asleep in Jesus; and those who remain will be caught up with them in the air.

Thank you, Father, for your resurrection promise. Because you overcame death, we look forward to being made both physically and spiritually whole at your Second Coming.

DAY 197

*Luke 12:4, 5 And I say unto you my friends, **be not afraid** of them that kill the body, and after that have no more that they can do. But I will forewarn you whom ye shall fear: fear him, which after he hath killed hath power to cast into hell; yea, I say unto you, fear him.*

No one can determine the destiny of a human soul except for our Redeemer, the judge of all the earth. Since this tent we reside in will eventually release our soul, Jesus kindly reminds His friends (covenant partners) that there is no cause for fear, because our real person is in His hands. He is the one to whom we should show a high regard and healthy respect.

Death is the ultimate fear for many on this earth, and yet there is something so much worse—eternal separation from you. Help me, Father, to keep a correct perspective concerning the two.

DAY 198

*Luke 12:7 But even the very hairs of your head are all numbered. **Fear not** therefore: ye are of more value than many sparrows.*

Jesus is giving His disciples proof that God is deeply concerned about every aspect of their lives. He loves us to such an extent that He gives a number to each hair on our head. Would you go to that extent for your children? Probably not, but God goes further. He left the glory of Heaven to become like us, "beset with our weakness," to become our source of salvation.

Father, you know more about me than I know about myself. You know what I can endure, what I can overcome, and what my future holds. Thank you that everything in my life has a purpose. I trust you will prepare me for it all.

DAY 199

Luke 12:32, 33 **Fear not**, *little flock, for it is your Father's good pleasure to give you the kingdom. Sell that ye have, and give alms; provide yourselves bags which wax not old, a treasure in the heavens that faileth not, where no thief approacheth, neither moth corrupteth.*

Many of our fears are based on our losing what this world has to offer, but Jesus said that is no reason to fear. He has a whole kingdom prepared to give us, and it brings Him great happiness to do so.

O Lord, how often I lose my focus. This world and its pleasures become so attractive to me, and it is but temporary. Help me to daily turn my heart toward home.

DAY 200

John 12:15 **Fear not**, *daughter of Sion: behold, thy King cometh, sitting on an ass's colt.*

This is a fulfilled prophecy of Zechariah 9:9. Every promise in God's Word has been, is being, or will eventually be fulfilled. The King came once to Jerusalem and they crucified Him. He will come again, and if we believe the truth of His Word, we have absolutely no reason to fear.

You, Lord, certainly do have the words of life. Help me to walk accordingly.

DAY 201

*John 14:27 Peace I leave with you, my peace I give unto you: not as the world giveth, give I unto you. Let not your heart be troubled, neither let it be **afraid**.*

Notice that it is our choice to be afraid. God did not leave us with a spirit of fear, but of peace. The world would describe peace as the absence of turmoil, whereas a Christian would describe a calmness and assurance that God is in control regardless of our circumstances.

Jesus, my heart will automatically be troubled if I let it. Thank you for this admonition that I should take the peace that you have given me to replace the fear that comes so naturally to my being.

DAY 202

*Acts 9:26 And when Saul was come to Jerusalem, he assayed to join himself to the disciples: but they were all **afraid** of him, and believed not that he was a disciple.*

It is natural to be afraid of what has caused us harm in the past. That's how we protect ourselves from being bruised, battered, and burned whether physically or emotionally. We do need to keep in mind, however, that God is capable of making great changes in people, and those who have bruised us in the past may be the bearers of future blessings.

I know that with you, Lord, all things are possible. May past bitterness never keep me from future blessings.

DAY 203

*Acts 18:9, 10 Then spake the Lord to Paul in the night by a vision, **Be not afraid**, but speak, and hold not thy peace: [10] For I am with thee, and no man shall set on thee to hurt thee: for I have much people in this city.*

When God tells us to speak, He has already prepared our audience. Whether it be a word of encouragement or of admonition, it is our responsibility to speak the truth in love. Paul had already experienced the presence of the Lord and knew that if Christ was with him there was nothing to fear.

I want to thank you, Lord, for putting your people beside me when you have asked me to speak. However, if you are not with me then I have nothing to say.

DAY 204

*Acts 22:9 And they that were with me saw indeed the light, and were **afraid**; but they heard not the voice of him that spake to me.*

Many see the light, and are in awe of His magnificence, but "faith cometh by hearing, and hearing by the Word of God." Who is in your circle of acquaintances that knows who God is but needs to hear His voice? Pray for them to do so, and determine if you are God's messenger to them.

Your Word says that the demons believe and tremble (James 3:19). Show me Lord, who it is that needs to hear your Word along with the light that they see.

DAY 205

*Acts 27:23-25 For there stood by me this night the angel of God, whose I am, and whom I serve, ²⁴Saying, **Fear not**, Paul; thou must be brought before Caesar: and, lo, God hath given thee all them that sail with thee. ²⁵Wherefore, sirs, be of good cheer: for I believe God, that it shall be even as it was told me.*

We will all encounter one or more shipwrecks in our lives. Even though angels are still working in our day it is more likely that we will receive our encouragement through the written Word and the power of His Holy Spirit. Paul could encourage others in this shipwreck because he knew to whom he belonged and he trusted the message as well as the messenger. If we are as sure of the promises in God's written Word, then we can say with Paul, "For I believe God, and it will be even as it has been written to me."

I do trust you as my protector, but I know that there are times when I need to trust you more fully. Thank you for your many promises to be with me and to prepare the way that I should go.

DAY 206

Romans 8:15 For ye have not received the spirit of bondage again to fear; but ye have received the Spirit of adoption, whereby we cry, Abba, Father.

119

Are you in bondage to anything? Does something besides God have a hold on your life? If so you can renounce it and let go because it is not from the One who promises to supply all of your needs. Jehovah Jireh, our provider doesn't treat us as slaves. He treats us as His very own children with a perfect love that casts out fear.

When fear comes calling—Abba Father! When the enemy entices me with temptation—Abba, Father! When I feel like I don't belong—Abba Father! Thank you for adopting me and making me secure.

DAY 207

Romans 11:20 Well; because of unbelief they were broken off, and thou standest by faith. Be not highminded, but fear…

"Behold both the kindness and the severity of God" verse 22 states. Israel should have recognized God's hand, but she closed her eyes to the Messiah. Therefore, the Gentiles were grafted in because of faith, not because of works. A healthy regard for His majesty and thanksgiving for His mercy is the perfect cure for high mindedness.

Realizing that I deserve nothing less than chastisement for my sin, I am in awe of your willingness to accept me with all my faults. Keep me, Lord, from self-sufficiency and arrogance.

DAY 208

Romans 13:3, 4 For rulers are not a terror to good works, but to the evil. Wilt thou then not be afraid of the power? Do that which is good, and thou shalt have praise of the same: ⁴ for he is the minister of God to thee for good. But if thou do that which is evil, be afraid; for he beareth not the sword in vain: for he is the minister of God, a revenger to execute wrath upon him that doeth evil.

Although God forbids us to take vengeance in our own hands, He often administers consequences for sin through our governing authorities. Paul actually called rulers "ministers of God." We should then have a healthy respect for the authorities that God has placed in our lives. If we choose to disobey the government we are disobeying God and have more than man to fear.

Thank you for placing me in a nation that considers the welfare of its citizens. I do not always agree with the decisions that are made, but I acknowledge that no one would be in authority over me unless it was given to them by you.

DAY 209

Philippians 2:12 Wherefore, my beloved, as ye have always obeyed, not as in my presence only, but now much more in my absence, work out your own salvation with fear and trembling.

God has worked within us a miracle beyond our comprehension. We are to evidence that to the world in our daily living. Let's not do this because someone might be watching, but by virtue of our sincere devotion to Christ Jesus.

The salvation that you have provided for me is too precious to be taken for granted. I want it to be so evident in my life that others see you before they see me.

DAY 210

*Colossians 3:22 Servants, obey in all things your masters according to the flesh; not with eyeservice, as menpleasers; but in singleness of heart, **fearing God**.*

Respect for God involves not only obedience to Him, but to the authorities He has placed in our lives. Notice that our attitude is as important as our actions. Whether we receive adequate compensation from man or not is of no consequence; we will receive our reward in full from God Most High.

Father, I don't always agree with my masters according to the flesh, and I have been guilty of following orders begrudgingly. Realizing that you see both the actions and the intents of the heart, I will ask that you make me aware of this quickly so as not to dishonor your name.

DAY 211

II Timothy 1:7 For God hath not given us the spirit of fear; but of power, and of love, and of a sound mind.

This is one of the most quoted verses related to fear in the Bible. Emphasize every word of this verse and think about its full implications. (*For* – Paul had just talked about the faith that was in Timothy and wanted to stir that up once again. *God* – He who knit us together in our mother's womb. *Hath not given* – If it did not come from God then imagine where it came from. *Us* – His beloved.) Continue in this manner and be extremely blessed.

Holy Spirit, you have been given to me by my beloved so that I have power, love, and a sound mind even in the most difficult circumstances. I accept all of these from you and ask that you would stir up such faith within me that when fear comes knocking we (the Holy Spirit and I) answer out of the abundance of these resources.

DAY 212

Hebrews 11:7 By faith Noah, being warned of God of things not seen as yet, moved with fear, prepared an ark to the saving of his house; by the which he condemned the world, and became heir of the righteousness which is by faith.

The story of Noah is a beautiful picture of salvation given to us in the Old Testament. We too have been warned of things not yet seen. We are moved by a respect for God and His Word to prepare our hearts unto salvation and become an heir of Christ's righteousness, not by our works, but by our faith as is seen in our works (ark building). Those who refuse do so will be condemned by their own neglect. No wonder the writer of Hebrews referred to Noah's faith.

Thank you, Lord, for the ark of salvation, for allowing us to be heirs of your righteousness, and for this healthy fear—respect for your sovereignty—which motivates us into action.

DAY 213

*Hebrews 11:23 By faith Moses, when he was born, was hid three months of his parents, because they saw he was a proper child; and they were **not afraid** of the king's commandment.*

There are times when the governing authorities violate God's instructions. At that point we must obey God rather than man. This should be done discretely and with respect. Starting riots is not God's modus operandi.

Help me, Father, to always discern between personal prejudices and biblical convictions. I would not want to dishonor your name for any reason. Empower me to live a life of faith even in the most difficult circumstances.

DAY 214

*Hebrews 11:27 By faith he forsook Egypt, **not fearing** the wrath of the king: for he endured, as seeing him who is invisible.*

Moses overcame his fear by focusing on the One who is invisible. That seems to be a paradox—focusing on what we cannot see. However, we are called on daily to *"Look not at the things which are seen, but at the things which are not seen: for the things which are seen are temporal; but the things which are not seen are eternal"(II Corinthians 4:8).*

Forsaking the world may be painful at the onset, but you have always made it worthwhile. The more I study your Word, the clearer my vision becomes and the more steadfast is my endurance.

DAY 215

*Hebrews 13:5, 6 Let your conversation be without covetousness; and be content with such things as ye have: for he hath said, I will never leave thee, nor forsake thee. So that we may boldly say, the Lord is my helper, and I will **not fear** what man shall do unto me.*

Even though man can hurt us physically, mentally, and emotionally, he can never separate us from the love of God (Romans 8:35-37). And God promises to work things for good in the lives of those who love Him (Romans 8:28). If you are convinced of these truths, allow them to seep out of your life continually.

Lord, you have been my helper, my strength, my provision, and contentment. May my lifestyle and my conversation boldly convey the fact that I trust you implicitly.

DAY 216
I Peter 2:17, 18 Honor all men. Love the brotherhood. Fear God. Honor the king. Servants, be subject to your masters with all fear; not only to the good and gentle, but also to the froward.

The persecution was probably intense for the "scattered" church during Peter's writing of this first letter, and Peter still insisted that Christians represent their Lord well by being good citizens. Notice that an inconsiderate authority in our lives does not release us from honoring or submitting to them. Our God is big enough to give us the grace to do what He has called us to do and will bless our obedience in the process.

Lord, you have never asked more of me than you have been willing to do yourself. When you were reviled, you reviled not in return; while suffering, you uttered no threats, but kept entrusting yourself to Him who judges righteously (I Peter 2:23). Give me the grace required to follow your example.

DAY 217
*I Peter 3:6 Even as Sara obeyed Abraham, calling him lord: whose daughters ye are, as long as ye do well, and are **not afraid** with any amazement.*

Although it took a few years for them to get this perfected, Sarah obeyed the Lord by being submissive to her husband. It is difficult for a woman to voluntarily place herself under the authority of a man, but we must remember that: *"the head of every man is Christ; and the head of the woman is the man; and the head of Christ is God" (I Corinthians 11:3).* We do well then, by trusting God to turn the head of the man so that we need not fear submissiveness.

Lord, it is much easier to get "under the mission" of an authority who has first submitted himself to you. In those instances where I disagree, help me to state my position and then trust you to turn his head toward your will.

DAY 218

*I Peter 3:14, 15 But and if ye suffer for righteousness' sake, happy are ye: and be **not afraid** of their terror, neither be troubled; [15] But sanctify the Lord God in your hearts: and be ready always to give an answer to every man that asketh you a reason of the hope that is in you with meekness and **fear**.*

Peter is only repeating what Jesus said in His "Sermon on the Mount." Blessed or "highly privileged" are those who hunger and thirst after righteousness, especially to the degree that they suffer because of their convictions. Others will ask where this uncommon loyalty originates, and we will then be able to share our respect for the Lord, and the hope that is within us.

Peter said that one of the keys to being without fear is sanctifying you in my heart again and again. I know he spoke from experience since he was put in the position to suffer for the sake of righteousness on more than one occasion. Help me to learn, even from the life of Peter, that the terror of men need not be a precursor to fear.

126

DAY 219

*Revelation 1:17, 18 And when I saw him, I fell at his feet as dead. And he laid his right hand upon me, saying unto me, **Fear not**; I am the first and the last: I am he that liveth, and was dead; and, behold, I am alive for evermore, Amen; and have the keys of hell and of death.*

Any time a human being comes into the presence of God we see a similar reaction. This sinful flesh cannot stand in the presence of such purity. Nevertheless, with His right hand of power, our Lord strengthened John and gave him the precious "fear not" command. Notice the verbs in Christ's message. Past tense: was dead. Present tense: **I am** the first and last; **I am** He that liveth; behold, **I am** alive for evermore; and **I have** the keys of hell and of death. Christ has taken care of the past, but our relationship with Him is much more about present and future certainties. *"Believest thou this?" (John 11:26).*

Thank you, Jesus, for taking care of my past, walking me through the present and preparing my future. Help me to live in the light of your promises and not my own inadequacies.

DAY 220

Revelation 15:4 Who shall not fear thee, O Lord, and glorify thy name? For thou only art holy: for all nations shall come and worship before thee; for thy judgments are made manifest.

Why do we honor, respect, and bow down to worship God? Because only He is Holy. There is none other in Heaven above or on earth below who deserves this type of reverence. This verse is but one more evidence of our triune God since Father, Son, and Spirit are all called Holy.

Yes, Lord, you only are holy and you only deserve our worship. All of your judgments are necessary and correct. You have been my rock and my fortress, my redeemer and my friend. Your very character demands that I refuse to entertain fear of another.

PART II

Secure In Christ

Many Christians live a life of doubt and fear because they are unsure of their position in Christ. The following verses reassure us that Christ's work on the cross is not a temporary work in the lives of those who trust Him as their personal Savior. It is a complete and continual work.

DAY 221

Romans 8:1, 2 There is therefore now no condemnation to them which are in Christ Jesus, who walk not after the flesh, but after the Spirit. [2] For the law of the Spirit of life in Christ Jesus hath made me free from the law of sin and death.

Just as the law of aerodynamics sets us free from the law of gravity, the law of the Spirit of life in Christ Jesus sets us free from the law of sin and death. We must, however, be a passenger in order to be set free from those laws which keep us attached to the earth. Rest assured that if you are *"in Christ Jesus"* then the law of the Spirit of life has set you free from condemnation.

My Savior, how thankful I am that you endured the curse of the law on my behalf and set me free. I choose to walk in the truth of "no condemnation" from this point forward.

DAY 222

Romans 8:38, 39 For I am persuaded, that neither death, nor life, nor angels, nor principalities, nor powers, nor things present, nor things to come, ³⁹ Nor height, nor depth, nor any other creature, shall be able to separate us from the love of God, which is in Christ Jesus our Lord.

Saints through the ages have experienced death, life, angels, principalities, powers, the height of joy, the depth of sorrow, deadly creatures and many other trials, but none of these have pulled a child of God out of His loving hand.

Lord, Paul was convinced of this truth because he had encountered much of what he wrote about in these two verses, yet his trials only served to draw him closer to you. May the things I encounter today serve only to draw me closer to my Jehovah Shammah, The LORD who is there.

DAY 223

John 10:27-29 My sheep hear my voice, and I know them, and they follow me: ²⁸ And I give unto them eternal life; and they shall never perish, neither shall any man pluck them out of my hand. ²⁹ My Father, which gave them me, is greater than all; and no man is able to pluck them out of my Father's hand.

What an outstanding promise from the lips of our Lord and Savior! There are so many key words in these verses that bring us assurance of Christ's intentions toward us and the Father's hold upon us: **My** sheep, **hear** my voice, I **know** them, they **follow** me, I **give** them **eternal** life, **never** perish, **greater** than all, my **Father's hand**. There is no safer place to be than in the hand of the one who knows you the best and loves you the most.

I hear you, Lord. You are speaking assurance to my heart this very moment. I am your lamb. I know your voice and have chosen to follow you accepting your gift of eternal life. My life is a gift to you, Jesus, from our Father. How freeing it is to know that no man can snatch us away from each other.

DAY 224

John 17:24 Father, I will that they also, whom thou hast given me, be with me where I am; that they may behold my glory, which thou hast given me: for thou lovedst me before the foundation of the world.

It is the will of Christ that we who have been given to Him by the Father spend eternity with Him beholding His glory. Since Jesus came to do the will of the Father (John 6:38) he always prayed within the will of the Father. It is as good as done.

Jesus, you paid the price, you prepared the place, and you prayed for grace on my behalf. I am looking forward to seeing you—face to face!

DAY 225

Hebrews 10:14 For by one offering he hath perfected forever them that are sanctified.

Under the Old Covenant, the high priests offered sacrifices day after day after day because their work was never completed. Christ, however, *took away the first in order to establish the second,* and our sin debt has been paid for all time.

Forgive me, Lord, for the times that I have taken your sacrifice lightly. I cannot fathom the weight of even my own debt, much less the sins of the whole world being placed upon your perfect body. It is your work that has made me secure, not my own.

DAY 226

Colossians 2:8-10 Beware lest any man spoil you through philosophy and vain deceit, after the tradition of men, after the rudiments of the world, and not after Christ. ⁹ For in him dwelleth all the fullness of the Godhead bodily. ¹⁰ And ye are complete in him, which is the head of all principality and power:

If we are not dwelling in the Word of God then we can easily be lead astray by false teachings and the traditions of men. We must check out every teaching and discover whether it is from man or from God. The truth is that Jesus Christ is God, and those who have personally accepted His work as High Priest and sacrifice are complete in Him.

The logic of man tells me that I must work in order to attain eternal life. Your Word tells me that you have completed the work. I choose to believe in your Word rather than man's reasoning.

DAY 227

Colossians 3:2-4 Set your affection on things above, not on things on the earth. ³ For ye are dead, and your life is hid with Christ in God. ⁴ When Christ, who is our life, shall appear, then shall ye also appear with him in glory.

Remember playing hide and seek as a child? Some children were easily discovered because they just could not bear to hide alone even for a few minutes. Life and death is certainly not a game, but I sure do like the fact that we are *hid with Christ in God* once we have died to self. I would say there is no better hiding place and no better company.

Why the world so often gets my attention Lord, I just do not understand. There is more satisfaction in you than anything the world has ever offered. Help me to delight in my position with you and not be anxious to see what everyone else is caught up in.

DAY 228

I Peter 1:3-5 Blessed be the God and Father of our Lord Jesus Christ, which according to his abundant mercy hath begotten us again unto a lively hope by the resurrection of Jesus Christ from the dead, ⁴ To an inheritance incorruptible, and undefiled, and that fadeth not away, reserved in heaven for you, ⁵ Who are kept by the power of God through faith unto salvation ready to be revealed in the last time.

Have you ever made reservations at a hotel or restaurant only to find upon arrival that there was a mix up and there is no room available? Our reservation for an inheritance was paid for by Jesus, accepted through faith, and is kept by the power of God. No wonder it can never fade, be corrupted, or defiled. There are more than a few benefits to knowing the Owner and His Son.

I may never dine with the elite upon this earth, Lord, or have much of an inheritance here; but oh how I look forward to entering the world's finest city, finding my place in the most spectacular dining hall, and being welcomed by the owner himself. Thank you for lavishing your grace upon one such as me.

DAY 229

Philippians 1:6 Being confident of this very thing, that he which hath begun a good work in you will perform it until the day of Jesus Christ:

The Apostle Paul was confident about many things, and this is but one reality he was able to observe in the lives of the many Christians he encountered: God is no quitter.

Father, I can think of many instances when I would have given up on a selfish saint like me, but you are oh so tenacious. I desire to resemble my Savior more and more every day even though the process is sometimes painful.

DAY 230

John 5:24 Verily, verily, I say unto you, He that heareth my word, and believeth on him that sent me, hath everlasting life, and shall not come into condemnation; but is passed from death unto life.

When something is passed from one owner to another there is often an exchange of title. When we hear God's truth and believe it for our own lives, we have a new owner. With this new owner comes all the benefits of the kingdom including everlasting life, no condemnation and no death. God will not relinquish a title that we have entrusted to Him.

I have heard your Word, I have trusted your work, and I have placed myself in your hands. I now rest assured that you will take very good care of your property.

DAY 231

Hebrews 7:25 Wherefore he is able also to save them to the uttermost that come unto God by him, seeing he ever liveth to make intercession for them.

The word *uttermost* combines the definitions both *completely* and *forever*. That is the extent of His work as our eternal High Priest. Are you not thankful that Christ does not do things halfway?

Lord, thank you for not disqualifying certain parts of my life when you took me in for regeneration. I trust that your work is progressing in my body, soul, and spirit even today as I make myself available to you.

DAY 232

John 3:16-18 For God so loved the world, that he gave his only begotten Son, that whosoever believeth in him should not perish, but have everlasting life. ¹⁷ For God sent not his Son into the world to condemn the world; but that the world through him might be saved. ¹⁸ He that believeth on him is not condemned: but he that believeth not is condemned already, because he hath not believed in the name of the only begotten Son of God.

God had every right to send His Son into the world to judge the world since we are all guilty of offending a most holy God. That judgment did take place when Christ took our sin in His body on the cross. *He was pierced for our transgressions; He was bruised for our iniquities.* That great exchange purchased eternal life for those who accepted His payment for their sins. He did not stop short in paying your debt, and neither will He hold back on the everlasting life He promised.

I have always known you to be a covenant keeping God. You have never fallen short of fulfilling any of your promises. I have believed in Christ's work on the cross, and I accept His gift of life without end.

DAY 233

Ephesians 1:13, 14 In whom ye also trusted, after that ye heard the word of truth, the gospel of your salvation: in whom also after that ye believed, ye were sealed with that holy Spirit of promise, ¹⁴ Which is the earnest of our inheritance until the redemption of the purchased possession, unto the praise of his glory.

When we hear the word of truth and respond to that word in faith by believing what Christ has done and trust Him for our salvation, then we are sealed with His Spirit. He is our guarantee that what God has begun will be completed. In the fullness of time we will receive our full inheritance which has already been purchased for us.

I am so thankful for the provision of the Holy Spirit in my life. He is my helper, my comforter, my guard, and my guide, bringing to my remembrance all that you have taught me. You thought of everything we would need and made those provisions for us. I stand amazed!

DAY 234

I John 4:12, 13 No man hath seen God at any time. If we love one another, God dwelleth in us, and his love is perfected in us. ¹³ Hereby know we that we dwell in him, and he in us, because he hath given us of his Spirit.

Since God is love and His Spirit dwells within every believer, a genuine love for others is an outpouring of God's character through us. It is but another confirmation of that mutual abiding relationship between God and His own.

Even though I cannot see you, God, I have experienced your presence in ways that are undeniable. I know that it is you loving through me when my flesh would naturally lash out towards someone or put up a barrier. Thank you for never putting up a barrier between you and me.

DAY 235

I John 5:13 These things have I written unto you that believe on the name of the Son of God; that ye may know that ye have eternal life, and that ye may believe on the name of the Son of God.

The book of *I John* is full of the evidence of God in the life of the believer. If there is any doubt at all that you are His child, immerse yourself in its five reassuring chapters. You will come across the word *know* approximately twenty-six times in your reading. If you are still unsure, now is a good time to give Him a place in every room of your "house".

Lord, Master, Savior, Owner, I give to you all that I am and all that I ever will be. Make me the vessel you have desired and then fill me with the fullness of your Spirit such that you spill out on all who come near.

PART III

My Indentity In Christ

You should be well on your way to freedom after spending 235 days exchanging your fears for a shield of faith. I would encourage you to stay the course and take up this additional armor which will establish you even deeper in the truth. These next verses remind us who we are in Christ so we can remind the enemy.

DAY 236

Galatians 5:1 Stand fast therefore in the liberty wherewith **Christ hath made us free**, *and be not entangled again with the yoke of bondage.*

Although Paul was actually referring to the yoke of the law which the Galatians had been enslaved by, this same principle applies to the yoke of fear or any other stronghold from which Christ has released us. We must persist in the Word daily so as not to get tangled up again with the lies of the enemy.

My Shield and my Defender, you are the One who has set me free. Thank you for purchasing my redemption certificate. I do not want to jeopardize my freedom by getting entangled again in a yoke of slavery. Help me recognize any yoke for what it truly is before it has a chance to entangle me. (Thank Him for the specific yokes from which He has set you free.)

DAY 237

*II Corinthians 5:17 Therefore if any man be in Christ, **he is a new creature**: old things are passed away; behold, all things are become new.*

Everyone enjoys getting something new do they not? However, it can be quite difficult to throw away the old because it's comfy and familiar. I like my old house, my old car, my old computer, my old tennis shoes, and my old jeans. When the old begins to deteriorate and no longer meets our needs, we must make an adjustment. Those of us who are in Christ must take off the old garment (filthy rags) and the old man (helpless, ungodly enemies of Christ) so we can put on the new robe of righteousness. If we leave the old stuff within reach we are likely to slip into it at times. Bury it and go on!

Lord, you have replaced my filthy rags with a robe of righteousness and made me a new creature. Forgive me for the times you have seen me trying on the old stuff again. It does not represent you well, and I would like to bury the whole wardrobe. (It might be helpful to make a list of the 'old things' that He has been trying to clean out of the closet.)

DAY 238

*Matthew 5:13 **Ye are the salt of the earth**: but if the salt has lost his savour, wherewith shall it be salted? It is thenceforth good for nothing, but to be cast out, and to be trodden under foot of men.*

Salt is a valuable and versatile substance whether it is used for seasoning, preserving, or healing. Since sodium chloride is necessary for the cells of the body to perform properly, our Creator gave warm-blooded animals a natural attraction to this compound. If we are salty Christians others will naturally be drawn to us as we are sprinkled throughout society adding flavor, preventing decay, and taking part in His healing process.

Creator God, Elohim, you have drawn me to yourself so that I could draw others to you. Work through me this day to preserve a soul, heal a broken spirit, or just add some flavor to someone's life. Sprinkle me where you will. (If He brings someone to mind, record the name and follow through.)

DAY 239

Matthew 5:14 **Ye are the light of the world**. *A city that is set on a hill cannot be hid.*

When Christ returned to the right hand of the Father, He chose to shine through those who would remain in the world. Together we are as a city, and the lights of that city are never more beautiful than when the darkness is the deepest.

You know, Lord, that I don't enjoy being in the dark. It is in those dark hours, however, that you have shown most brightly in my life. Set me where you will and shine brightly through me.

DAY 240

Romans 1:6, 7 Among whom **are ye also the called** *of Jesus Christ:* [7] *To all that be in Rome, beloved of God, called to be saints: Grace to you and peace from God our Father, and the Lord Jesus Christ.*

We who have come to Christ have come because we were called. We were not only called to someone, we were called to something. Paul reminded the believers in Rome that they were called to be saints—set apart for an intended purpose. All the resources needed for our duties, including grace and peace, are freely given by God our Father and the Lord Jesus Christ.

All I have needed, Lord, you have provided. Great is your faithfulness to those you have called. May I be just as faithful in the responsibilities to which I have been called. (List a few of those responsibilities and recommit them to His will.)

DAY 241

*Romans 5:1, 2 Therefore being **justified by faith**, we have peace with God through our Lord Jesus Christ: ² By whom also we have access by faith into this **grace wherein we stand,** and rejoice in hope of the glory of God.*

I can think of no better explanation for *justified* than the one I have heard since childhood, "Just as if I had never sinned." That absolutely astounds me since I know that I am a sinner and would have no peace or place with God were it not for my access through Jesus Christ.

I am standing in grace: God's Righteousness At Christ's Expense. I have reason to rejoice and hope. Knowing that none of this is deserved, Father, makes it all the more precious.

DAY 242

*Romans 6:11, 12 Likewise reckon ye also yourselves to **be dead indeed unto sin, but alive unto God** through Jesus Christ our*

Lord. [12] Let not sin therefore reign in your mortal body, that ye should obey it in the lusts thereof.

Whether it is fear or other sins with which we have struggled, we must count them as inactive and inoperable elements of our past. God is willing to exert His power in our life now, but we must give place to Him constantly and no longer give place to the lust of the flesh, lust of the eyes, or the pride of life.

Looking back over my life, Father, I realize that neither fear nor any other sin has ever brought life to me, and yet I am still tempted at times to disobey your instructions by trying to protect this flesh of mine or offer it a little pleasure. I would ask you to prompt me very quickly by the power of your Spirit before I am allowed to act apart from you in any way. (Continue to journal what you feel He is speaking to your spirit concerning each passage, and review your notes often.)

DAY 243

*Romans 14:8 For whether we live, we live unto the Lord; and whether we die, we die unto the Lord: whether we live therefore, or die, **we are the Lord's.***

We are all accountable to a variety of people in our lives whether it be to our spouse, our children, our employer, friends, or members of organizations to which we belong. Ultimately, however, in life and in death, we are accountable to the Lord. Not only can this free us, but it can also liberate others whom we feel the need to judge.

What freedom comes along with this truth! There are those in this life that I will never please, but not so with you, Lord.

Therefore, that will be my focus today—being a servant who pleases my master.

DAY 244
*I Corinthians 1:9 God is faithful, by whom **ye were called unto the fellowship of his Son** Jesus Christ our Lord.*

Think for a moment how you would respond if secular royalty called you into their inner circle of fellowship. Should we respond with any less enthusiasm to the King of all kings?

Father, you have proven yourself faithful over and over again, faithful to call and faithful to answer. The invitation to fellowship with your very own Son far outweighs any opportunity we could ever experience on this earth. Help me today to enjoy the full aspects of fellowship available to me through Jesus Christ.

DAY 245
*I Corinthians 1:30, 31 But **of him are ye in Christ Jesus,** who of God is made unto us wisdom, and righteousness, and sanctification, and redemption: ³¹ That, according as it is written, he that glorieth, let him glory in the Lord.*

Are you tempted to make comparisons between yourself and other believers? Have you ever felt shortchanged in the area of giftedness? Even though you may still be in the process of discovering your specific spiritual gifts, rejoice in the fact that you have received the most pertinent gifts showered by Christ on all believers: wisdom to replace foolishness, righteousness substituted for guilt, redemption from the slave market of sin, and ongoing sanctification through the work of the Holy Spirit.

Oh Father, thank you for supplying all I need according to your riches in glory in Christ Jesus: wisdom, righteousness, sanctification, and redemption. I desire to please you with the resources you have made available to me, but let me not glory in anything outside of my personal relationship with you.

DAY 246

I Corinthians 2:16 Now we have received, not the spirit of the world, but the spirit which is of God; that we might know the things that are freely given to us of God. [13] Which things also we speak, not in the words which man's wisdom teacheth, but which the Holy Ghost teacheth; comparing spiritual things with spiritual. [14] But the natural man receiveth not the things of the Spirit of God: for they are foolishness unto him: neither can he know them, because they are spiritually discerned. [15] But he that is spiritual judgeth all things, yet he himself is judged of no man. [16] For who hath known the mind of the Lord, that he may instruct him? **But we have the mind of Christ.**

What a wonderful truth! If you have received Christ as your personal Savior, then His wisdom is made available to you today through the power of the Holy Spirit! Think about it: never to be without the wisdom of the One who created this universe and keeps it running. Of course, it is up to each of us individually to allow His thinking to override our own.

Jesus, I need your instruction. My own wisdom is flawed. I am weak and you are strong. Impart to your servant today wisdom mixed with humility, compassion seasoned by discernment,

145

and an unwavering determination to fulfill the purposes you have for me today.

DAY 247

*I Corinthians 3:9 For **we are labourers together with God**: ye are God's husbandry, ye are God's building.*

Even though we are God's field which He is cultivating and His building being built up together in Christ, He allows us to work with Him as co-laborers. As soon as we confess our sins and trust Christ as our personal Savior, He puts us to work seeding, watering, fertilizing, harvesting, and drawing others into the wonderful shelter of His grace and forgiveness. If you feel useless, you need to check in with the building and grounds director. You are needed somewhere in the field.

Father, thank you for creating a job suited to my skills, talents, gifts, and abilities. I enjoy co-laboring with you. I know you remember as well as I do those assignments I thought I could handle on my own. They were quite unproductive.

DAY 248

*I Corinthians 3:16, 17 Know ye not that **ye are the temple of God**, and that the Spirit of God dwelleth in you? [17] If any man defile the temple of God, him shall God destroy; for the temple of God is holy, which temple ye are.*

Under the Old Covenant, God instructed Solomon to build a house for His name. God said that His eyes and His heart would be there perpetually as long as His people did not turn away from and forsake His commandments to serve other gods (II Chronicles 7:16-22). God was faithful to His word in that when they turned to other gods, the temple was destroyed. Under the New Covenant, God dwells in His temple, believers in Christ, by means of His Holy Spirit. He is no less concerned about His house today than He was in Solomon's day. It is up to each of us to keep His sanctuary holy and undefiled.

Jesus, as I read your prayer for the present day temple of God (John 17:20-26), I stand in agreement. It is my desire that your glory shine through this temple in such a way that the world would have absolutely no doubt that it is your dwelling place.

DAY 249

*I Corinthians 3:21-23 Therefore let no man glory in men. For all things are yours; ²² Whether Paul, or Apollos, or Cephas, or the world, or life, or death, or things present, or things to come; all are yours; ²³ **And ye are Christ's**; and Christ is God's.*

God has made available to us great teachers along with priceless resources for our personal growth and the furtherance of the gospel. We must be careful not to boast in these gifts nor take them for granted. Of more value than all these is the fact that we are Christ's and Christ is God's. There is no room for coveting here!

Father, thank you for all the great teaching you have made available to me throughout my lifetime. I know the purpose for these gifts remains exactly as Jesus expressed it in John 17:23, "I in them, and Thou in Me, that they may be perfected in unity, that the world may know that Thou didst send Me, and didst love them, even as Thou didst love Me." It is my desire to join Christ in this endeavor.

DAY 250

*1 Corinthians 6:17 But he that is **joined unto the Lord** is one spirit.*

Whatever we join ourselves to becomes a part of us, and we become a part of it. As followers of Jesus Christ, we have become one with Him taking Him everywhere we go. Is He comfortable in your surroundings? Does the Spirit of Christ rejoice as you converse with friends, family, co-workers and acquaintances? In light of this reminder, should you make any adjustments?

It is good to be reminded that you are with me at all times, Lord, that my spirit is your dwelling place. Create in me a clean heart, Oh God, and renew a right spirit within me.

DAY 251

*1 Corinthians 6:19, 20 What? Know ye not that **your body is the temple of the Holy Ghost** which is in you, which ye have of God, and ye are not your own? 20 For ye are bought with a price: therefore glorify God in your body, and in your spirit, which are God's.*

There is no doubt that our intricately woven bodies are an amazing work of God. Jesus Christ redeemed these bodies with the blood of His own, and the Holy Spirit dwells within to guide and direct. We are His by plan, by purchase, and by presence.

Why do I try to exercise my rights when in reality I should defer to you in all things? The only rights I have are the ones you obtained for me. Show me now, Lord, if I am allowing your temple to be defiled in any way.

148

DAY 252

*I Corinthians 7:22 For he that is called in the Lord, being a servant, is the **Lord's freeman**: likewise also he that is called, being free, is **Christ's servant**.*

In this life we all will serve someone or something. By choosing to serve Christ, we enter into a glorious freedom regardless of our external state. It is a freedom, however, that delights in pleasing the master.

You have set me free from so many things, Lord Jesus: free from helplessness, hopelessness, blindness, impurities, guilt, shame, condemnation, destruction, death, and countless fears. How could I ever desire less than total devotion to the One who has rescued me and set me free?

DAY 253

*II Corinthians 1:4 Who comforteth us in all our tribulation, that we may be able to comfort them which are in any trouble, by the comfort wherewith **we ourselves are comforted of God**.*

Tribulation is a part of life. It causes us to grow and makes us useable to others as we bring them to the One who has been our comfort in affliction.

Wonderful Counselor, thank you for being with me through every tribulation. Even during the darkest times of my life you have provided a reassurance of your sovereignty. Help me to be faithful in completing the cycle of comfort, drawing others to your healing side.

DAY 254

*II Corinthians 1:21, 22 Now he which stablisheth us with you in Christ, and hath anointed us, is God; ²² Who hath also **sealed us, and given the earnest of the Spirit in our hearts.***

An official will often place his seal on his possessions so all who see the seal will know that the product is genuine. The saints of God carry the seal of the Holy Spirit upon their lives. He is the evidence of authenticity signifying that we are His for now and for all eternity.

Signed, sealed, and waiting to be delivered. I have no reason to doubt the authenticity of your Word, Lord. May I provide others no reason to doubt the authenticity of my salvation.

DAY 255

*II Corinthians 2:14 Now thanks be unto God, which always **causeth us to triumph in Christ**, and maketh manifest the savour of his knowledge by us in every place.*

Paul was most likely thinking of the Roman triumph which was used to honor conquering generals. In this processional the commander in chief would ride in a golden chariot surrounded by his officers and followed by the conquered enemy. The approach of the processional was revealed by the odor of incense which was an important element of every triumph.

Thank you, Jesus, for conquering Satan, sin and even myself. As I follow you in victory it is my desire to bear the sweet aroma of the knowledge of you in every place.

DAY 256

II Corinthians 2:15, 16 For **we are unto God a sweet savour of Christ**, *in them that are saved, and in them that perish:* [16] *To the one we are the savour of death unto death; and to the other the savour of life unto life. And who is sufficient for these things?*

Think for just a moment about the past twenty-four hours. Are you pleased concerning the aroma you left in every place? Were you an encouragement to the saved and a window to the lost? If you did not walk in triumph yesterday, determine to triumph in Christ today!

Who is sufficient for these things, Lord? Certainly it is not me. I make myself available to your Spirit today and ask that you would seep out of me and into the world.

DAY 257

II Corinthians 3:3 Forasmuch as **ye are manifestly declared to be the epistle of Christ** *ministered by us, written not with ink, but with the Spirit of the living God; not in tables of stone, but in fleshy tables of the heart.*

While we are a letter being written, we are also a writing instrument through which the Spirit of the living God must flow. How freely is the Spirit flowing through you? Does your writing tip get stiff and stubborn from lack of use? Do you need to be shaken up or heated every now and then so that the Spirit can once again flow freely? Maybe you have an agenda of your own, leaving unsightly blobs of ink all over the place. Regardless of what we have been like in the past, if we are sincerely available to His adjustments, He will make sure that the marks left behind represent Him well. Our job is to be available and willing to be adjusted.

You wrote a beautiful message upon my heart, and now I want to be a free-flowing pen available for the Spirit's use at a moment's notice. Clean out the clutter and put me to good use.

DAY 258

II *Corinthians 3:6 Who also hath made us **able ministers of the new testament**; not of the letter, but of the spirit: for the letter killeth, but the spirit giveth life.*

Paul is explaining a great difference between the old covenant and the new. The old covenant could not give life since none could live up to God's standards. Conversely, the new covenant gives life to those who accept Christ's righteousness as their own access to the Father. We preach the new covenant message to the world around us as we allow the Holy Spirit to make us fit for the kingdom.

Father, I have been guilty of expecting perfection from both myself and others. It is not my intent to live under the old covenant. Help me to rely more on your grace and extend the same to others.

DAY 259

II *Corinthians 3:18 But **we all**, with open face beholding as in a glass the glory of the Lord, **are changed into the same image from glory to glory**, even as by the Spirit of the Lord.*

Have you noticed that after several years of marriage, a husband and wife tend to resemble each other, not only in attitude and actions, but even in physical appearance? It is intended to be the same with the bride of Christ. As we spend time in the presence of our bridegroom, others should notice a striking resemblance.

Jesus, there could be no greater compliment than to hear someone say that I resemble the lover of my soul. I expect you would take pleasure in the same. Thank you for the ministry of your Spirit who is working on that assignment even now.

DAY 260

II Corinthians 4:1 Therefore seeing **we have this ministry***, as we have received mercy, we faint not...*

I am eternally grateful that Jesus Christ did not give up at the most difficult moment of his earthly ministry. He never said, "Father, I just can't do this anymore!" Why? Because He was willing to be a channel of blessing flowing from the Father to the most needy of all creatures regardless of the cost.

Father, you have chosen me to be a channel of blessing to someone today. Even if I never know who it is, would you transfer through me your love, joy, peace, patience, kindness, goodness, gentleness, faithfulness and mercy like a smooth flowing stream? I'm available.

DAY 261

II Corinthians 4:7 But **we have this treasure in earthen vessels***, that the excellency of the power may be of God, and not of us.*

Why would God choose to place the richest of all treasures in a fragile earthen vessel? It is the nature of the container that makes it ideal: fragile, dirty, and created specifically to be filled.

Creator God, you have made me to be a container of your glory, broken and mended many times over. The only excellence, the only power I have ever known has been manifest when this vessel was empty of self. Help me to stay clutter free so that nothing conceals the brilliance of your glory.

DAY 262

*II Corinthians 4:8-10 We are troubled on every side, yet not distressed; we are perplexed, but not in despair[b]; [9] Persecuted, but not forsaken; cast down, but not destroyed; [10] Always bearing about in the body the dying of the Lord Jesus, **that the life also of Jesus might be made manifest in our body.***

Can you identify? Have you been troubled on every side: pressed, mistreated, discouraged, and without understanding? Rest assured that the Master Carpenter knows exactly how to prepare His building materials. And in order to cut, press, sand, and stain your section of His masterpiece, He must hold you in His powerful, loving hands.

Lord, as you hand carve this component of your kingdom, I trust your perfect judgment submitting myself to your tender touch.

DAY 263

*II Corinthians 4:16, 17 For which cause we faint not; but though our outward man perish, yet **the inward man is*** *renewed day by day.* ¹⁷ *For our light affliction, which is but for a moment, worketh for us a far more exceeding and eternal weight of glory.*

Have you ever lived in a house during renovation? It is a most unpleasant experience always taking longer than expected. Nevertheless, while the old things are being removed and the dust is flying, we remind ourselves of what is to come so as not to abandon the work before completion.

Father, we have gone through some very long "moments" together. This project would surely have been abandoned if I were the supervisor. Thank you for your vision where mine has been shortsighted.

DAY 264

II Corinthians 5:1 For we know that if our earthly house of this tabernacle were dissolved, **we have a building of God, an house not made with hands, eternal in the heavens**.

I love the way the Apostle Paul reminds believers to maintain a heavenly perspective while dwelling on the earth even when considering our physical body. A tabernacle or tent is often used in scripture as a metaphor for the human body since both are temporary dwelling places. One day our earthly tent will be irreparable, and we will leave it behind for an indestructible house which is better suited for eternity.

Elohim, when you created this physical body in which my soul resides. you did so with great care and wisdom, and yet it was meant to be disposable. I can only imagine the detail and love being put into my eternal house prepared to dwell in the presence of my Savior.

DAY 265

*II Corinthians 5:7 For **we walk by faith, not by sight**.*

Our Sovereign Lord has seen fit to allow us the pleasure of faith while we sojourn on this earth. He could very easily have given us more information about our heavenly home, and even more details about this life. He chose instead to give us just enough information that we must trust Him for what we do not see. Faith is a requirement for those who are in Christ Jesus.

I admit, Lord, that I often wish you had given us more details about our heavenly home, and sometimes I would like to hear an audible voice for direction and reassurance. On the other hand, I know you have given me all that is necessary to live a life pleasing to you, and I ask for discernment as I continue walking.

DAY 266

*II Corinthians 5:18 And all things are of God, who hath reconciled us to himself by Jesus Christ, and **hath given to us the ministry of reconciliation**...*

God would never ask us to do anything to which He has not already committed Himself including the extremely difficult task of reconciliation. No matter how hard we think it is to follow His example in this matter, we can go to the cross and find all the strength we need.

Father, how thankful I am that you had a plan for reconciliation from the foundation of the world. I cannot imagine what it would be like to live my life with a chasm of disharmony between us. Is there disharmony anywhere in my life that I need to address today?

DAY 267

*II Corinthians 5:20, 21 Now then **we are ambassadors for Christ,** as though God did beseech you by us: we pray you in Christ's stead, be ye reconciled to God.* [21] *For he hath made him to be sin for us, who knew no sin; **that we might be made the righteousness of God in him**.*

An ambassador legally represents the person of his or her sovereign. He is commissioned with at least one specific task to be carried out with the desire and integrity of the one who gave him authority. Christ carried out God's work of revealing the Father and reconciling mankind to Himself by paying our sin debt. He has now appointed us to be His own ambassadors. And what if it costs us a little to do the job as commissioned? Our full debt has been paid.

Lord, may I no longer consider the cost to me but remember the debt from which I've been freed.

DAY 268

*II Corinthians 9:8 And God is able to make **all grace** abound toward you; that ye, **always** having **all sufficiency** in **all things**, may **abound to every good work**:*

Has the Holy Spirit put a good work on your heart? Have you been wondering where the resources or the strength will come from to accomplish this particular task? Although He may appoint others to help with the assignment, our dependence must be upon Him. He has **all** we need.

Today, Lord, I make myself available to you. I will need your grace and sufficiency for all things if a good work is to be accomplished. I realize that true success is measured by the

157

obedience and trust produced in the lives of those who call you Master.

DAY 269

*II Corinthians 10:4, 5 (For **the weapons of our warfare are not carnal, but mighty through God** to the pulling down of strong holds;)* ^{5} *Casting down imaginations , and every high thing that exalteth itself against the knowledge of God, and bringing into captivity every thought to the obedience of Christ;*

As a shepherd boy David did not need the armor of King Saul to defeat Goliath; it was cumbersome and ineffective. Likewise, the weapons of the world are of no use to God's children fighting in the battlefield of the mind. We must rely on the armor supplied by our commander in chief: Salvation, Truth, Faith, Righteousness, God's Word, the Gospel of Peace, and Prayer.

Father, I will stand firm having put on the helmet of salvation, buckled my belt of truth, and allowed you to cover my vital organs with your breastplate of righteousness. I have soaked my shield of faith in the water of your Word so as to quench all the fiery darts of the evil one. I will use the sword of the Spirit as Jesus exampled for me in the wilderness while I walk through this world sharing the gospel of peace. I commit myself once again to be on the alert with prayer at all times in the spirit for all the saints.

DAY 270

*Galatians 2:20 **I am crucified with Christ**: nevertheless I live; yet not I, but **Christ liveth in me**: and the life which I now live* *in the flesh I live by the faith of the Son of God, who loved me, and gave himself for me.*

How can one be crucified and yet live? It is only possible by that amazing power God used to raise Christ from the dead and seat Him at His right hand in the heavenly places. The life of faith defers to Christ and receives resurrection power day by day, moment by moment.

Father, since the time that I agreed to be crucified with Christ, I chose to live by the faith of your Son who loved me and gave himself for me. Daily I require your transfusion of faith, power, love and life flowing through my inner man.

DAY 271

*Galatians 3:24-26 Wherefore the law was our schoolmaster to bring us unto Christ, that we might be justified by faith. ²⁵ But after that faith is come, we are no longer under a schoolmaster. ²⁶ **For ye are all the children of God by faith in Christ Jesus**.*

What a wonderful truth Paul was teaching the church of Galatia! Our relationship to the Father does not depend upon our works; rather, we are justified by faith in Christ's work. By this we are made children of the Master Creator, motivated by love rather than by law.

Schoolmaster Law was harsh at times, Lord, but oh how necessary for me to see myself against the backdrop of your perfection. I needed the schoolmaster to unveil the truth of my sin and lead me to the One who could make me clean. Since you have cleansed me and loved me, I want no other gods in my life. Since you have caused me to love others, I also want your best for them. Thank you for making me your child.

159

DAY 272

Galatians 3:29 And if ye be Christ's, then are ye Abraham's seed, and **heirs according to the promise.**

What is your inheritance as a child of Abraham? Paul explained in *Galatians 3:6-9* that the righteousness reckoned to Abraham because of his faith would also be credited to those who believe as Abraham believed, fully entrusting themselves to God. This justification and right standing before God brings with it a New Testament full of blessings.

You have been showing me, Father, the blessings that are mine in Christ. I too consider everything as loss compared to the surpassing greatness of knowing Christ Jesus my Lord.

DAY 273

Galatians 4:6, 7 And because ye are sons, God hath sent forth the Spirit of his Son into your hearts, crying, Abba, Father. [7] **Wherefore thou art no more a servant, but a son***; and if a son, then an heir of God through Christ.*

Can you imagine how distressing it would be to have a child that obeys and serves only out of duty with no desire to draw near for fellowship, advice, comfort, strength, or wisdom? It would probably break your heart, just as it hurts deeply the heart of our Heavenly Father when His children treat Him in such a manner. Therefore, He gives us His Spirit, living within, craving for us the most intimate, personal relationship that a child could have with a parent. To circumvent that relationship would be to grieve the Holy Spirit of God.

LORD, we are both aware of the fact that there are days when I treat you as Master but not as Father. Please forgive my thoughtlessness! May I no longer grieve your Spirit by being insensitive to your desire for my fellowship.

DAY 274

*Galatians 5:22, 23 But the **fruit of the Spirit** is love, joy, peace, longsuffering, gentleness, goodness, faith, ²³ Meekness, temperance: against such there is no law.*

Herein lies the difference between one who enjoys fellowship with the Father and one who serves only out of obligation. Although much work may be accomplished by a dedicated servant, fresh, beautiful, abundant fruit can only be produced in the life of one who abides in the Vine.

I desire fruit, Father, fresh, beautiful fruit that entices others to visit the Vine and meet the Vinedresser.

DAY 275

*Ephesians 1:1 Paul, an apostle of Jesus Christ by the will of God, **to the saints** which are at Ephesus, and to the faithful in Christ Jesus…*

You do not have to leave this earth to be a saint, but you do have to die. When you chose to be crucified with Christ (death to self), you were also raised up with Him and spiritually seated in heavenly places. A natural result of death to self and a new, heavenly vantage point is faithfulness in Christ Jesus.

Lord, you have made me a saint. I realize that it is my responsibility to be faithful to the calling to which I have been called. I need an added measure of power in the area of…

161

DAY 276

Ephesians 1:2 **Grace be to you, and peace***, from God our Father, and from the Lord Jesus Christ.*

What blessed gifts originate from God our Father and Jesus our Lord! If God were not our Father, or if Jesus were not our Lord, neither grace nor peace would be possible. Keep in mind also that grace must be accepted by each of us individually before we will ever experience true peace.

Oh that I might never take these blessed gifts for granted!

DAY 277

Ephesians 1:3 Blessed be the God and Father of our Lord Jesus Christ, who hath **blessed us with all spiritual blessings in heavenly places in Christ:**

Though our home is in heaven, all the blessings of our citizenship are available to us today. We accept them at salvation and need only to appropriate them as we continue this earthly journey.

Holy Spirit, give me the courage to walk in the blessings of my citizenship. I confess, Lord, that in some areas I have lived like a pauper even though I am a child of the King.

DAY 278

Ephesians 1:4 According as he hath **chosen us in him** *before the foundation of the world, that we should be holy and without blame before him in love...*

Who: The Sovereign LORD of the entire universe
What: chose us

Where: in Christ
When: before the foundation of the world
Why: that we should be holy and blameless before Him
How: in love

What wonderful treasures you have put within this particular scripture, Father. I am both humbled and in awe of you choosing me.

DAY 279

*Ephesians 1:5 Having **predestinated us unto the adoption** of children by Jesus Christ to himself, according to the good pleasure of his will...*

You have never been and will never be an unwanted child; it was God's pleasure to adopt you into His family. In fact He has been working on this adoption plan since before the creation of the universe. It was necessary for this adoption to go through a mediator since reconciliation between the adopter and adoptee was required. The mediation process was the most treacherous on the mediator Himself, but He persevered and we are the beneficiaries of His determined love.

Never has a mediator endured so much in order to accomplish reconciliation. Thank you for your desire to have me as your own, for drawing me with lovingkindness, and funding the adoption transaction with your own blood.

DAY 280

*Ephesians 1:6 To the praise of the glory of his grace, wherein he hath made us **accepted in the beloved.***

God's grace is glorious; so glorious in fact, that he made you and me, who were so filthy with sin, accepted in His perfect kingdom. This could never happen outside of grace, outside of a great exchange: Christ's robe of righteousness for our filthy rags. The phrase, *"to the praise of His glory,"* occurs three times in the first chapter of Ephesians referring first to the adoption of the saints, then to the sanctification of the saints, and finally to the final inheritance of the saints.

Father, Son, and Spirit, may my life be a thanksgiving for the adoption, sanctification, and inheritance you have graciously made available to me. I give myself to you in return to the praise of the glory of your grace.

DAY 281

*Ephesians 1:7 In whom **we have redemption through his blood**, the forgiveness of sins, according to the riches of his grace…*

What is redemption? It is the process of buying back or freeing one from captivity by payment of a ransom. We were all slaves to the cruel Master Sin with no hope of achieving liberation except through the blood of one who had never known sin. This perfect redeemer would have to accept the punishment for each individual transgression committed by every slave He wanted to purchase. The punishment would come with utter humiliation and the most extreme physical, mental, and emotional pain ever known to humanity. Christ agreed to the terms, became the redeemer, humbled himself, and paid the price – His blood for your freedom. Could anyone possibly reject the ultimate redemption sacrifice in favor of serving Master Sin?

I accept your redemption! How could I not? May I be as willing to share the riches of grace and forgiveness with others as you have been to share the riches of your grace and forgiveness with me.

DAY 282

*Ephesians 1:11 In whom also **we have obtained an inheritance**, being predestinated according to the purpose of him who worketh all things after the counsel of his own will: [12] That we should be to the praise of his glory, who first trusted in Christ.*

Perhaps you have received or will some day receive an inheritance of worldly value or could it be that you've been overlooked or cheated out of an inheritance in one way or another. All of that may seem very important while we operate in this material world. However, rest assured, your real inheritance was allotted to you at the time of your salvation and no sibling, lawyer, or judge can revoke what God has predestined.

I am both humbled and honored to be included in so great a heritage. Show me any area in my life, Lord, that is not to the praise of your glory.

DAY 283

*Ephesians 1:13 In whom ye also trusted, after that ye heard the word of truth, the gospel of your salvation: in whom also after that ye believed, **ye were sealed with that holy Spirit of promise,***

The phrase, "signed, sealed, and delivered" comes to mind when we read this verse. Our covenant was signed with the blood of Jesus Christ. We are sealed by the Holy Spirit of Promise, and we will be delivered into the presence of the Father when our task on this earth is complete.

Lord, I have heard your word of truth, the gospel of my salvation. I have believed and am ever grateful for the proof of your presence by the seal of your Spirit upon my life.

DAY 284

Ephesians 2:4, 5 But God, who is rich in mercy, for his great love wherewith he loved us, ⁵ Even when we were dead in sins, **hath quickened us together with Christ,** *(by grace ye are saved;)*

All of us were at one time considered "the living dead." We may have had blood pumping through our body, but there was no real life in our spirit. We were insufficient to correct the problem. Only one–the Author of Life–has the authority to make a dead man live again, and out of His great love for us He did just that. We are not only alive, but we are alive together with Christ! This means that there will never be true life without Christ. We are given life at salvation, and we manifest the sweet aroma of His life in our daily existence.

Merciful Father, thank you for the great love with which you have loved me. I remember what it was like to be dead in my transgressions, always searching but never finding true fulfillment. Now that I have been made alive together with Christ, I want to manifest the sweet aroma of the knowledge of you in every place.

DAY 285

*Ephesians 2:6 And **hath raised us up together**, and **made us sit together in heavenly places in Christ Jesus**:*

We are the reason that God raised Christ up from the dead. He was raised so that we could join Him in heavenly places, physically in the future, but spiritually in the present. This position should change our point of view concerning what is happening in and around us each and every day. Are you living according to an earthly or a heavenly perspective?

I admit, Lord, that I so often get bogged down in this world looking at things from my distorted point of view. Help me to see each person and every situation I encounter today from your perspective.

DAY 286

*Ephesians 2:8, 9 For **by grace are ye saved through faith**; and that not of yourselves: it is the gift of God: ⁹ Not of works, lest any man should boast.*

God has made available to each of us the gift of salvation by grace. It is accepted through faith in what Christ has done for us personally. Although we cannot work to pay for this gift, our gratefulness is expressed through a life which brings honor to the One who purchased it for us.

Father, it is only by your grace that I have been given life. Help me this day to be a reflection of that grace in the life of another.

DAY 287

*Ephesians 2:10 For **we are his workmanship**, created in Christ Jesus unto good works, which God hath before ordained that we should walk in them.*

When I am called upon to complete a task, I like to do as much preparation work ahead of time as is possible because it makes the task much more manageable. God has called each of us for specific tasks in His kingdom, but He did not leave us on our own to accomplish those tasks; in fact, He began the preparation work even before we were born. We have each been given special gifts, talents, and personalities to match our calling. If you mistakenly thought those gifts were to be used for your advancement, you need only to come to Him with a repentant heart and ask Him to do some restructuring in your life.

Oh, Father, I am guilty of selfishly using the gifts, talents, and abilities with which you have blessed me. Please forgive me and continue your work of sanctification in my life so that I am found to be a trustworthy steward of your blessings. I want to walk in the path that you have before ordained for my life not the path of least resistance.

DAY 288

*Ephesians 2:13 But now in Christ Jesus ye who sometimes were far off **are made nigh by the blood of Christ.***

Before the establishment of the New Covenant in Christ Jesus, we Gentiles were strangers to the promise, having no hope, and without God (Ephesians 2:12). But Christ removed the barrier by becoming our reconciliation. Now we who once were far off are as near to God as we choose to be.

168

Today, Father, I need to feel your nearness. As fully as I know how, I submit myself to you body, soul, and spirit. Make me completely yours. Satisfy my longings and quench my thirst.

DAY 289

*Ephesians 2:14 For **he is our peace**, who hath made both one, and hath broken down the middle wall of partition between us...*

Christ is the master carpenter, but He is also a master of demolition. He has removed wall upon wall to draw you near to Himself, and He longs to tear down the walls of partition that you have built up against others. The first several bricks are removed by prayer. Take that difficult relationship to the throne of grace. Christ will meet you and help you intercede for those whose names may be difficult to even speak aloud.

Holy Spirit, kneel with me here before the throne. I am oh so weak and tired of allowing my mind to be cluttered with this barrier. I bring _____ before your throne, Father God. Help me to see this one through your eyes. Tear down walls of hate and distrust. Replace them with mercy and compassion. I submit myself to you, the master builder.

DAY 290

*Ephesians 2:18 For through him **we both have access** by one Spirit unto the Father.*

What used to be the privilege of one priest from one nation on one day of the year is now open to all those who come in the name of Jesus Christ. You have constant access to the heavenly throne room with the accompaniment of the Spirit to speak to God the Father at any time you choose.

Jesus, thank you for your sacrifice that gives me access by the Spirit to the Father. I never want to take this privilege for granted or forget the price you paid to give me this freedom.

DAY 291

*Ephesians 2:19 Now therefore ye are no more strangers and foreigners, but fellow citizens with the saints, and **of the household of God**...*

We once traveled to Stockholm, Sweden, and were on our own for the first 24 hours. Boy, did we feel like strangers in a strange place! But as soon as our Swedish friends arrived we were made to feel right at home, as if we were part of their own precious family. Jesus arrived on the scene to bring all who were strangers to the covenant into the household of God and give them heavenly citizenship. Each of us must choose, however, if we will accept His gracious invitation or continue a life of wandering.

I remember well my wanderings, Lord. Thank you for rescuing me and making me part of your Father's household.

DAY 292

*Ephesians 3:12 In whom **we have boldness and access with confidence** by the faith of him.*

Can you imagine what would have happened if a child had followed the high priest into the Holy of Holies on the Day of Atonement? The results would have been terribly tragic for all of Israel. Yet a child of God can boldly enter the Holy of Holies today with confidence through the access given us by our high priest, Jesus Christ.

Father, each time I enter your presence you make me feel more than welcome. Not only do you allow me to speak directly to you, but you consistently permeate my heart with words of encouragement. Thank you for the confidence you have given me to come before your throne.

DAY 293

*Ephesians 3:16 That he would grant you, according to the riches of his glory, to be **strengthened with might by his Spirit in the inner man**...*

If I were to give you a gift according to my riches, then your endowment would be in direct proportion to my wealth. Likewise, it is in direct proportion to Christ's riches that the power of the Holy Spirit is made available to our inner man. Do you need more power to be Christ-like in attitude and actions? His riches will cover the cost.

Holy Spirit, since my outward person is decaying and my inner person is being renewed, we should be winning more and more battles against the flesh. Forgive me for the battles that we forfeit because the flesh comes with ample resources while my inner person thinks she can go it alone.

DAY 294

Ephesians 3:17-19 That Christ may dwell in your hearts by faith; that ye, being rooted and grounded in love, [18] May be able to comprehend with all saints what is the breadth, and

*length, and depth, and height; [19] And to know the love of Christ, which passeth knowledge, **that ye might be filled with all the fullness of God.***

While in the prayer room at our church, my daughter and I were both using my Bible to pray the prayers of Paul over our congregation. Ephesians is so marked and highlighted in my Bible that it is now difficult to read. Bria prayed, "Lord, may they be booted to the ground in love." After a bit of laughter we decided that it very well could have been a Holy Spirit inspired blunder. Sometimes God has to knock our legs right out from under us so that we can be emptied of self and filled with all the fullness of God.

Lord, we both know how often I have been booted to the ground in love. Thank you for doing what is necessary to teach me the breadth, length, depth, and height of your love. Fill me to overflowing, O God.

DAY 295

*Ephesians 3:20 Now unto him that is able to do exceeding abundantly above all that we ask or think, **according to the power that worketh in us…***

We tend to forget that we have a power source working within us which enables us to do things that only God could imagine. The problems begin when we go at such a pace that we become disconnected with the power source and try to substitute with alternative sources of energy—none on which Christians were designed to run. At that point we are doing more harm than good to ourselves and others. We desperately need to stay connected.

172

Lord, I want my life to be one of exceeding abundance. Help me to discern quickly when I am running on alternative sources of power so that I do not destroy the work that you have already accomplished.

DAY 296

*Ephesians 4:7 But **unto every one of us is given grace** according to the measure of the gift of Christ.*

All who have eternal life have been given the gift of salvation through His grace as a result of our faith. The beautiful thing about being in the body of Christ is that the gift giving did not stop with eternal life. He has also given each of us spiritual gifts (grace gifts) that enable us to function in the church just as remarkably as our physical body parts fit and function together. As a newborn it takes time and practice to figure out how all of these parts operate as a team to accomplish what the brain desires, and so it is with His body, the church. Grace has been given to make it possible, and with a little patience and practice we will be walking in a manner worthy of our calling.

Your grace, Lord, truly is amazing in so many ways. Thank you for salvation by grace through faith, for the grace gifts that bring joy with the service, and for your daily grace in giving me much more than I ever deserve. Help me to be a grace giver rather than a grace grabber.

DAY 297

*Ephesians 4:24 And that ye **put on the new man**, which after God is created in righteousness and true holiness.*

173

When Christ comes to take over a life He lovingly begins to reveal Himself to us, in us, and through us. His character is the new man that we are to put on. It is through the emptying of self that His Spirit becomes more visible in us. He came at the point of salvation; self departs through the process of sanctification, and when our flesh is no longer an issue, that will be glorification.

I'm ready to lay aside the old self which is corrupted by fear, anger, jealousy, selfishness, and unforgiveness, along with all manner of unkind thoughts and deeds. Consume me today, Lord, with your righteousness and true holiness.

DAY 298

*Philippians 1:6 Being confident of this very thing, that **he** which **hath begun a good work in you** will perform it until the day of Jesus Christ…*

If you have confessed with your mouth that Jesus is Lord and have believed in your heart that God has raised Him from the dead, (Romans 10:9) then Christ has begun a good work in you. The work of salvation fuels the work of sanctification which continues until glorification. Whatever He is doing in your life right now is part of His wonderful plan to manifest the sweet aroma of the knowledge of Him in every place (II Corinthians 2:14) so that others will make themselves available to that same good work.

My confidence is growing, Lord, but you know that it has taken me quite some time to come to this place of daily making myself available for your good work. Thank you for working in me and not expecting me to do this on my own.

DAY 299

*Philippians 1:11 **Being filled with the fruits of righteousness**, which are by Jesus Christ, unto the glory and praise of God.*

Jesus Christ, the Righteous Branch, told His disciples that if we abide in Him we will bear much fruit, but apart from Him we can do no good thing. Is it your plan to abide and continue being filled with the fruits of righteousness this day? Or have you decided to disconnect and have a go of it on your own? You choose—abide and see God glorified, or disengage and have a fruitless day.

Jesus, I choose this day to be a fruitful branch. I'm anxious to see what you have in store.

DAY 300

*Philippians 1:21 For to me **to live is Christ**, and to die is gain.*

What do you think comes to the mind of your friends and family when your name is mentioned? Does it have anything to do with Christ? Our Creator certainly wants us to enjoy the life we have been given, but in the process of living, we miss life itself it we have lived for self.

I consider your grace, Lord Jesus, that though you were rich, you became poor so that through your poverty I might become rich. That makes death a gain to me. May my life be a gain to you.

DAY 301

Philippians 2:13 **For it is God which worketh in you** *both to will and to do of his good pleasure.*

If you have a desire to be pleasing to God today, it is because God is working His will within you. If your only desire is to please self, try submitting your will to His, and then stand amazed at what He can accomplish through you.

You have said, Lord, that I am your workmanship created in Christ Jesus to do things which you have prepared beforehand (Ephesians 2:10). I trust that you are working in me and for me (Romans 8:28) to accomplish what you desire to do through me.

DAY 302

Philippians 4:12, 13 I know both how to be abased, and I know how to abound: everywhere and in all things I am instructed both to be full and to be hungry, both to abound and to suffer need. **I can do all things through Christ which strengtheneth me***.*

The apostle Paul had learned how to get along with whatever God had made available to him at any certain time. Paul focused on working for God and God took care of working for Paul.

When my body is satisfied, I want to be hungry for you. When my body is in need, I know that your grace abounds. May my roots forever run deep into your well of living water. Strengthen me for your work today.

176

DAY 303

*Philippians 4:19 But my **God shall supply all your need** according to his riches in glory by Christ Jesus.*

What is man's greatest need? It is not more education; it is not more programs; and it is not wealth. Man's greatest need is Jesus. When that need is met, everything else will fall into place.

Paul called you his God, and it is a privilege to call you my God also. You have faithfully supplied all my needs beginning with my need for a Savior. Colossians 2:3 reminds me that in Christ are hidden all the treasures of wisdom and knowledge. When I have Christ, I have everything. Thank you, Jehovah Jireh, for your abundant provision.

DAY 304

*Colossians 1:12-13 Giving thanks unto the Father, which hath made us meet to be partakers of the inheritance of the saints in light: [13] **Who hath delivered us from the power of darkness, and hath translated us into the kingdom of his dear Son:***

Christ is called our Savior because He paid the ransom to deliver us from the power of darkness and translate us into the kingdom of light. What may have been a relatively simple transition for us was all but simple for the Father, the Son, and the Holy Spirit. Thank God today for His indescribable gift.

Father, I realize that you have qualified me to be a partaker of the inheritance of the saints. No amount of preparation, training, or work on my part would grant me that freedom. What is a privilege to me caused great pain for my Lord. May my life continually show my gratitude for your indescribable gift.

DAY 305

Colossians 1:14 In whom **we have redemption** *through his blood,* **even the forgiveness of sins**…

We have redemption. Sounds somewhat like, "We have liftoff!" does it not? In fact there are some similarities between the two: No longer does the world have a hold on us; the law of the Spirit of life in Christ Jesus has set us free from the law of sin and death. We have embarked on a great adventure, a mission for the Lord Jesus Christ, and we now have the ability to see all of life from a heavenly perspective.

Jesus, thank you for paying the price of my redemption, setting me free, forgiving my sin, and securing my future. Help me to see my world today from your perspective.

DAY 306

Colossians 2:10 And **ye are complete in him**, *which is the head of all principality and power*…

The Bible does not teach that we need Jesus plus something else in order to be complete. All that is needed for life and godliness is supplied through our all-sufficient Savior. What we may need however, is a lesson in appropriating His provision.

Most of my life, Lord, I have felt incomplete in one aspect or another. Thank you for this reminder that I am complete in you. I trust that you will continue to empower me this day and prepare me for the days ahead.

DAY 307

*Colossians 2:12 **Buried with him** in baptism, wherein also ye are **risen with him** through the faith of the operation of God, who hath raised him from the dead.*

The ordinance of baptism in the life of a believer is a beautiful illustration of what has happened in the inner man. Through the waters of baptism we are identifying with Christ in His death, burial, and resurrection. Notice that all of this is *"through the faith of the operation of God."*

Thank you, Father, for the ordinance of baptism which serves as a testimony to others and a reminder to me that since I have been symbolically buried with Christ, I will also be raised with Him to everlasting life. Empower me to walk today in that newness of life.

DAY 308

Colossians 2:14 Blotting out the handwriting of ordinances that was against us, which was contrary to us, and took it out of the way, nailing it to his cross...

Not only was Christ nailed to the cross, but the ordinances that kept us from the blessings of covenant were also pierced through on that bittersweet day. Christ blotted out all that stands between man and God. If there is an obstruction in your relationship with the Father, it is not from His estate. He has cleared all obstacles and is waiting for each of us to walk in the grace of full access.

Thank you Lord for blotting out all that stands in the way of full access to you. I choose to live today not under the domain of the law but under the domain of Christ.

DAY 309

Colossians 3:3, 4 For ye are dead, and **your life is hid with Christ in God**. *⁴ When Christ, who is our life, shall appear, then shall ye also appear with him in glory.*

Take a good look at your life today. Who is often hidden and who is more likely to be revealed, you or Christ? Our anonymity will not last forever though; when Christ appears, we will appear with Him in glory. I would much rather be revealed in His glory than in my own flesh wouldn't you?

Remind me today, Holy Spirit, to consider myself hidden within the shelter and security of the Most High. I desire to abide in the shadow of the Almighty. When I am joyful, sad, angry, or weary, may Christ be revealed while I stay concealed.

DAY 310

Colossians 3:9, 10 Lie not one to another, seeing that ye have put off the old man with his deeds; ¹⁰ And **have put on the new man**, *which is renewed in knowledge after the image of him that created him…*

Our society constantly conceals truth or exaggerates it. The media calls those who do so "spin doctors," but God calls them liars. The Apostle Paul reminds us that lying is a remnant of the old nature trying to resurface through the new. The Bible reminds us that God is not a man that He should lie, so if we take every thought captive to the obedience of Christ we can stop ourselves before we begin to "spin."

Father, Your Word is truth. As I meditate on your Word daily I ask that you would sanctify me in truth. I pray in agreement with your Son who has already asked for this on my behalf. Remind me to take every thought captive so that the new man is revealed and the old man is not only concealed but shriveled up to nonexistence.

DAY 311
*I Thessalonians 2:12 That ye would walk worthy of God, **who hath called you unto his kingdom and glory.***

Where God reigns His glory is obvious. If The Great I AM is the ruler of your life then His glory will be visible through you. If you reign supreme in your own life then God's glory will be concealed. Will you choose today to be a window or a self portrait?

Father, your kingdom come, your will be done in my life as it is in heaven. Allow others to see your glory through me today.

DAY 312
*1 Thessalonians 4:9 But as touching brotherly love ye need not that I write unto you: for **ye yourselves are taught of God to love one another.***

With the institution of the New Covenant God promised to be our personal instructor (Jeremiah 31:31-34). This personal teaching is referred to in I John 2:20, 27 as an unction or an anointing from the Holy One. Who else but God could teach us to love one another as He loves us? If I choose then to be unloving, I am not only quenching the Spirit of God in my life, I am also grieving Him (Ephesians 5:30).

God, I know how frustrating it can be to give instruction that goes unheeded. I have often been a stubborn student, selfishly following my own agenda and hurting others in the process. I present myself to you once more as a pupil ready to receive instruction.

DAY 313

*I Thessalonians 4:17 Then we which are alive and remain shall be caught up together with them in the clouds, to meet the Lord in the air: and **so shall we ever be with the Lord**.*

We will always be—a promise from the infallible Word of God. Being is good, but being with the Lord, now that is awesome!

Creator, Sustainer, Resurrected Lord, thank you for the triune gift of life. You formed me in my mother's womb, you saved me from the ravages of sin, and you have promised life everlasting beyond what I can comprehend. Creation, Salvation, and Resurrection—your miracles, my riches in Christ Jesus.

DAY 314

*I Thessalonians 5:5 **Ye are all the children of light**, and the children of the day: we are not of the night, nor of darkness.*

If you are a child of the day, you will respond to light. If you are a child of the night, darkness will peak your interest. What a tragedy it is to be given sight and yet be unresponsive to "The Light of the World."

Light of Life, Light of Men, I am reminded that when you came to this earth, darkness could neither apprehend nor overcome your radiance. May I be a true reflection of you as I encounter both children of the day and of the night.

DAY 315

*I Thessalonians 5:9, 10 For God hath not **appointed** us to wrath, but **to obtain salvation by our Lord Jesus Christ,** Who died for us, that, whether we wake or sleep, we should live together with him.*

The Apostle Paul reminds believers at Thessalonica, along with all others who read this letter, that God did not appoint us to wrath. Christ, on the other hand, was the Lamb of God slain from the foundation of the earth. God intended to place the entirety of His wrath for our sin upon Jesus Christ so that we could obtain salvation. How tragic it is that so many refuse their substitute, thereby choosing to experience the wrath of God themselves.

I am once again reminded that you are too holy to overlook sin. How grateful I am that my sin was paid for at the cross. Help me to be a faithful steward of the mysteries of God as I share this awesome truth with others.

DAY 316

*I Thessalonians 5:23, 24 And **the very God of peace sanctify you wholly**; and I pray God your whole spirit and soul and body be preserved blameless unto the coming of our Lord Jesus Christ. Faithful is he that calleth you, who also will do it.*

It was Christ who imputed righteousness to us, and it is Christ who will present us *"with no spot or wrinkle, or any such thing, holy and blameless"* before the throne. Is life a little uncomfortable at the moment? Sanctification is rarely smooth sailing, but keep in mind that Jehovah Mekoddishkem (I AM your Sanctifier) is also Jehovah Shalom (I AM your peace).

Jehovah Shalom, it is your faithfulness and peace that empower me to move forward when the sanctification process is most difficult. I continue to submit my spirit, soul, and body to your perfect work. Thank you for continuing the work you began in me.

DAY 317

*II Thessalonians 2:13 But we are bound to give thanks always to God for you, brethren **beloved of the Lord**, because God hath from the beginning chosen you to salvation through sanctification of the Spirit and belief of the truth...*

The English transliteration of the word "beloved" here is *agapao*. It is that unselfish love that has its birth in the heart of God and flows into the lives of His children. It is this love that Paul describes to the church at Corinth as being patient, kind, not easily angered, and keeping no record of wrongs. It is this type of love which always protects, always hopes, always perseveres, rejoices with the truth, and never fails. It is the "why" and the "how" of His choosing you to take part in salvation.

I have experienced this agapao from your heart, Father. You were patient, kind, gentle, and protective of me before I ever knew you. You brought me out of the pit and placed me on solid ground. Your love has abounded toward me still more and more since that time. I believe your truth and rejoice in your salvation.

DAY 318
II Thessalonians 3:3 But the Lord is faithful, **who shall stablish you, and keep you from evil**.

What a promise for the one who calls Jesus Lord! The word *"stablish"* means to make stable, to strengthen, make firm, and to render constant. It is our Lord's stability, strength, and constant presence in our lives that will keep us from evil.

Lord Jesus, you are The Faithful One. It is my desire to be established, strengthened and made constant by you, through you, and for you. Although the enemy is seeking to catch me off guard today, I trust that my feet are set on the Solid Rock, and you have rendered him powerless where I am concerned.

DAY 319
II Timothy 1:7 For **God hath** *not* **given us the spirit of** *fear;* *but of* **power, and of love, and of a sound mind.**

We know what God has not given us—a spirit of fear. Although what He has given us is just as important: a spirit of **power**, *dunamis*, from which we get our word dynamite; of **love**, *agape,* which was born in the heart of God and flows into the hearts of His children; and of a **sound mind**, *sophronismos*, moderation, sound judgment, and self discipline. So we have dynamic power with which to accomplish anything He asks of us together with His love and discipline. Are you possessing your possessions today, or are they unclaimed gifts waiting to be opened and put to good use?

185

This day, Lord, I will need your dynamic power to overcome temptations, to move into places that are uncomfortable for me, and to speak the truth in love to myself and others.

DAY 320

*II Timothy 1:9 Who hath **saved us, and called us with an holy calling**, not according to our works, but according to his own purpose and grace, which was given us in Christ Jesus before the world began.*

"Called with a holy calling…" Do you ever feel like you need to apologize for your position in Christ? You may be ridiculed by the world for who you are and what you stand for, but never forget that your calling is a holy calling from a holy God who has prepared you beforehand to take part in His redemptive plan. There is no greater calling.

It was by grace you saved me through faith, not through any works of righteousness that I have done. However, I know that I was created in Christ Jesus for good works. It is my desire to work out what you have been working in me.

DAY 321

*II Timothy 1:12 For the which cause I also suffer these things: nevertheless I am not ashamed: for **I know whom I have believed** and am persuaded that he is able to keep that which I have committed unto him against that day.*

The great reward of following Christ is that we know **whom** we have believed. Whether in plenty or in want, sorrow or great joy, it is the "whom" of our belief that persuades us. What you believe is important, but if Jesus Christ is not the "whom" in your spiritual beliefs then they are of no value for eternity.

Jesus, thank you for revealing yourself as "The Way, The Truth, and The Life." I am persuaded that you are able to keep that which I've committed unto you against that day.

DAY 322

*II Timothy 4:8 Henceforth **there is laid up for me a crown of righteousness**, which the Lord, the righteous judge, shall give me at that day: and not to me only, but unto all them also that love his appearing.*

Are you looking forward to Christ's appearing – that day when He receives His bride unto Himself? The forward look is a product of a Philippians 1:21 mindset – *"For to me, to live is Christ, and to die is gain."* The antithesis of which we must steer away is the Philippians 2:21 mindset – *" For all seek their own, not the things which are Jesus Christ's."*

You, Lord, are righteous and holy and forgiving. It is because of your first appearing that I can look forward to the second. Remind me to keep the Philippians 1:21 mndset and steer clear of the Philippians 2:21 trap so that you make daily appearances through my life.

DAY 323

Titus 2:13, 14 Looking for that blessed hope, and the glorious appearing of the great God and our Savior Jesus Christ; [14] Who gave himself for us, that he might redeem us from all *iniquity, and purify unto himself **a peculiar people, zealous of good works.***

"She/he is a bit peculiar" may not be a compliment in the world's economy, but in God's economy it is a tribute resulting from our purification. The work we do as a peculiar people identifies us as such and stands as proof that we love Him, that we are looking forward to the glorious appearing, and desire others to experience peculiarity also.

I look forward to your glorious appearing because you are just, righteous, merciful, and faithful to your promises. I realize that the only truly good work done in regard to salvation is the work you completed when you said, "It is finished." May gratitude for your work of grace be evident in my life today.

DAY 324
*Titus 3:7 That being **justified by his grace**, we should be made **heirs according to the hope of eternal life.***

Many times in the New Testament our Lord reminds us that we are heirs of eternal life made so by the transfer of **G**od's **R**ighteousness **A**t **C**hrist's **E**xpense. How do we say, "Thank you" to the One who gave His life in exchange for ours? We do so by laying aside our own will in exchange for His.

Life eternal is so hard for me to comprehend, Lord; even more difficult to fathom is the pain and rejection you experienced in order for me to be accepted. A heavenly perspective precludes any striving for praise, power, or prestige on this side of eternity.

188

DAY 325

*Hebrews 1:14 Are they not all ministering spirits, sent forth to minister for them who shall be **heirs of salvation**?*

God has ordained that His ministering spirits, the angels, attend to the heirs of salvation. While we should never focus on the angels, we can be thankful that our Father will use all His resources to guide, guard, and grow us while we press on to *"the upward call of God in Christ Jesus."*

I read in the scriptures, Lord, of how your angels nourish, protect, deliver, rejoice over, and carry believers to their eternal home. I am mindful that you are Jehovah Sabaoth—the LORD of Hosts. Thank you for the unseen hands that have nourished, protected, delivered, and rejoiced over me as your child. I look forward to the opening of my eyes when I am transported into your presence.

DAY 326

*Hebrews 3:1 Wherefore, **holy brethren, partakers of the heavenly calling**, consider the Apostle and High Priest of our profession, Christ Jesus.*

Those who profess Christ Jesus as their Savior and High Priest are themselves considered holy, partakers of the heavenly calling. We declare this heavenly citizenship and maintain our joy by communicating with the Maker of heaven, speaking with the grace of heaven, keeping the perspective of heaven, appropriating the power of heaven, and participating in the business of heaven—the summing up of all things in Christ Jesus.

Today, Lord, I submit myself to your cause. May I speak words of grace, see others through your eyes, and be a transmitter of your power.

DAY 327

*Hebrews 3:6 But Christ as a Son over his own house; **whose house are we**, if we hold fast the confidence and the rejoicing of the hope firm unto the end.*

We are the body of Christ, the dwelling place of God on this earth. Is the light on in His house today? Is His house inviting and welcoming all who would desire to rest with Him? Is the front porch clean and the pathway clear? Are there portraits of the Savior in His house? Are the words spoken in His house edifying, giving grace to those who hear?

I realize, Lord, that the way your house is maintained is evidence of ownership. May my life, your house, be inviting in every way to those who would come. Show me this day your personal preferences for your dwelling place.

DAY 328

*Hebrews 3:14 For **we are made partakers of Christ**, if we hold the beginning of our confidence steadfast unto the end.*

We are "made partakers of Christ"—partners with Christ. He has done a work in you so that He can do a work through you. Do you plan to work with Him or against Him today? The reality of this partnership is proven by our continuance in the faith. What God has joined together, let no man put asunder.

I am your partner today, Lord. Since you are the way, the truth, and the life, I will be looking and listening for your guidance. Lead on!

DAY 329

Hebrews 4:3 For **we which have believed do enter into rest,** *as he said, As I have sworn in my wrath, if they shall enter into my rest: although the works were finished from the foundation of the world.*

What a wonderful promise for those who believe God—REST! The word "believed" in this passage speaks of commitment, not just mental assent. As we commit more of ourselves to the Sovereign Creator and Ruler of the universe, we experience more of His rest.

My steadfast hope for eternity rests in your completed work while my hope for this day rests in your ongoing work in me and through me. I give to you at this moment all those situations that could invade my peace and steal my joy.

DAY 330

Hebrews 4:14 Seeing then that **we have a great high priest, that is passed into the heavens,** *Jesus the Son of God, let us hold fast our profession.*

Every phrase in this powerful verse is essential to our salvation, reminding us who we are and what we have in Christ Jesus. The biblical priests spoke to God on behalf of the people, but only the Great High Priest was able to thoroughly, perfectly, and eternally bridge the gap between God and man. We can hold fast and hold forth our profession because the One who has passed into the heavens is holding us.

Seeing then that you are my Great High Priest, who has passed into the heavens making intercession for me, I will move forward in confidence this day.

DAY 331

*Heb. 4:15 For we have not an high priest which cannot be touched with the feeling of our infirmities; but was in all points tempted like as we are, yet without sin. [16] Let us therefore come boldly unto the throne of grace, that **we may obtain mercy, and find grace to help in time of need.***

Mercy, not getting what we deserve, and grace, receiving what we do not deserve, are priceless and essential treasures purchased for us by the work of our High Priest. Be aware of what they cost our Lord and take them not for granted.

You alone know my greatest need, the desire of my heart for this day. May your grace and mercy flow through me into the lives of others so that what cost you your life will be multiplied in mine.

DAY 332

*Hebrews 7:24, 25 But this man, because he continueth ever, hath an unchangeable priesthood. [25] Wherefore **he is able also to save them to the uttermost that come unto God by him**, seeing he ever liveth to make intercession for them.*

The Greek word for "uttermost" can also be translated completely, perfectly, entirely, forever, or to the end.

192

Because the priesthood of Jesus Christ continues forever, His intercession is without end. He has provided my salvation and will continue to provide my salvation perfectly, entirely, and forever.

Jesus, you are my Prophet, my Priest, and my King. Thank you for your continual intercession which allows me to stand blameless before the throne of God. I want to join in your work today by interceding on behalf of_____.
May this one receive a glimpse of your glory and be forever changed.

DAY 333

Hebrews 10:19-22 Having therefore, brethren, **boldness to enter into the holiest by the blood of Jesus,** *[20] By a new and living way, which he hath consecrated for us, through the veil, that is to say, his flesh; [21] And having an high priest over the house of God; [22] Let us* **draw near with a true heart in full assurance of faith, having our hearts sprinkled from an evil conscience, and our bodies washed with pure water.**

It is through the veil not around the veil that we enter the holy place of God. No amount of self-confidence, self-sacrifice, or even self-loathing will allow communication with the sovereign ruler of the universe. Nevertheless, those who have been cleansed by the blood of Christ may draw as near as they desire. Will you approach God's throne with hesitation or boldness today?

It is in you, Jesus Christ, that I am able to enter the holy place. Confident that your pure life and sacrificial death have paved the way for me to approach the Most High, I desire to draw very near. Search me, O God, and know my heart; try me and

193

know my anxious thoughts; see if there is any wicked, hurtful way in me and lead me in the everlasting way.

DAY 334

*Hebrews 12:1 Wherefore seeing **we also are compassed about with so great a cloud of witnesses**, let us lay aside every weight, and the sin which doth so easily beset us, and let us run with patience the race that is set before us...*

Heroes of faith, many described in Hebrews 11, have gone before us enduring hardship while pressing toward that city and that kingdom promised by our covenant-keeping God. They, in essence, cheer us on to persist in the race set before us. We, likewise, will influence others in this generation and the next. Will you be identified by the generations as a hero of faith?

I desire to follow your instruction for induction into the hall of faith laying aside every weight and the sin which so easily besets me so as to run with endurance the race in which you have called me to participate. Thank you for your great faithfulness to previous generations and to my own.

DAY 335

*Hebrews 12:9, 10 Furthermore we have had fathers of our flesh which corrected us, and we gave them reverence: shall we not much rather be in subjection unto the Father of spirits, and live? ¹⁰ For they verily for a few days chastened us after their own pleasure; but he for our profit, that **we might be partakers of his holiness**.*

The subject of discipline is rarely something that brings a smile to our face, and yet it is God's profitable tool for growth in our lives. We soon discover that our heavenly Father will not leave those He loves without discipline, but neither will He leave us in discipline.

Since we are encouraged to count it all joy, I want to thank you for not turning your back on me when admonition is in order. Drawing close to you during times of correction lessens the pain immensely.

DAY 336

Hebrews 12:28, 29 Wherefore we **receiving a kingdom which cannot be moved**, *let us have grace, whereby we may serve God acceptably with reverence and godly fear: [29] For our God is a consuming fire.*

What does the Bible classify as enduring? God's faithfulness, God's mercies, God's Word, God's kingdom, spiritual food, spiritual rewards, faith, hope, love, and other things which are unseen by the human eye (II Corinthians 4:18). Do you want to know what is truly stable in your life? Turn everything over to the consuming fire.

Father, even though I do not enjoy being shaken, it is in those times of testing that you define the eternal and the temporal. Open my eyes to see the gold, silver, and precious stones so that I do not waste this precious life working for wood, hay, and stubble.

DAY 337

*Hebrews 13:5, 6 Let your conversation be without covetousness; and be content with such things as ye have: for he hath said, I will never leave thee, nor forsake thee. ⁶ So that we may boldly say, **The Lord is my helper**, and I will not fear what man shall do unto me.*

What is the key to contentment? Understanding that your Father owns everything you could ever need and has promised not only be your supply, but also to help you manage what He has given.

You, Lord, are my helper and my gracious supply. It is your faithfulness that enables my boldness. Show me where I've bowed to the king of covetousness in my life and help me turn so that I bow to you alone.

DAY 338

*James 1:5 **If any of you lack wisdom, let him ask of God, that giveth to all men liberally**, and upbraideth not; and it shall be given him.*

Once again the scripture reminds us to ask and we shall receive. Inspired by the very Spirit of God, Paul told the Colossians that in Christ are hidden all the treasures of wisdom and knowledge. His letter to the Philippians also reminds us that God will supply all our needs through His riches in glory in Christ Jesus. Our Designer, Creator, and Sustainer is delighted to give out of His riches to those whom He created to show forth His glory. The only conditions are to realize our need and humbly ask.

How needy I am Lord and how abundant is your supply. I'm asking for your magnificent, merciful, and manifold wisdom. Help me see my circumstances today from your point of view so as to agree with the intercession of Christ.

DAY 339

I Peter 1:3, 4 Blessed be the God and Father of our Lord Jesus Christ, which according to his abundant mercy hath **begotten us again unto a lively hope** *by the resurrection of Jesus Christ from the dead,* [4] **To an inheritance incorruptible, and undefiled, and that fadeth not away, reserved in heaven for you.**

How lively is your hope? Is your daily testimony spirited and energetic as you live in anticipation of your promised inheritance? Keep in mind that eternal reservations made through Jesus Christ are personally guaranteed by Him to be free from corruption, defilement, and fading. You will be recognized from afar and given a grand reception upon arrival. You are strongly encouraged to invite all your friends, family, and acquaintances to join you.

Father, thank you for your abundant mercy. I realize that I have often allowed my lively hope to become lethargic and uninspiring. Forgive me for taking this magnificent inheritance for granted. Who shall I invite to join me in the kingdom today?

DAY 340

I Peter 1:5 Who are **kept by the power of God through faith unto salvation** *ready to be revealed in the last time.*

197

Consider today the continuous, unfailing power of God that is keeping you from evil, temptation, persecution, dangers, calamities, and most importantly keeping you for the glory that is to be revealed in the last day. As Jesus said, *"Neither shall any man pluck them out of my hand. My Father, which gave them me, is greater than all; and no man is able to pluck them out of my Father's hand."* Praise Him for his keeping power.

Omnipotent God, I choose to dwell in your shelter and abide in your shadow this day. You are my refuge and my fortress. You have delivered me from the snare of the trapper and from the deadly pestilence. Your faithfulness is a shield and a buffer.

DAY 341

*I Peter 1:15, 16 But as he which hath called you is holy, so **be ye holy in all manner of conversation;** [16] Because it is written, Be ye holy; for I am holy.*

God's holiness is exhibited in His thoughts, His words, His actions, and in every aspect of His character. Think about your last twenty-four hours. Did your thoughts, words, actions, and other aspects of your character reflect the holiness of the One who called you out of darkness into His marvelous light? Ask the Holy Spirit to bring this passage to your mind throughout the day and then surrender your thoughts, words, actions, and entire character to Him.

Lord, you are righteous in all your ways, holy in all your works. I surrender my thoughts, my words, my actions, my character to you today. I acknowledge my areas of weakness and trust that you will nudge me in my spirit when I'm tempted to overlook your commands.

DAY 342

*I Peter 1:23 Being **born again, not of corruptible seed, but of incorruptible**, by the word of God, which liveth and abideth for ever.*

Whatever is born of the flesh will most certainly decay, whether it be our physical bodies or the works of the flesh. But that which is born of the Spirit has come by faith, through the hearing of the Word, and will not see corruption. As you hear the Word of God today, allow the Spirit to do an abiding work in you and through you.

Holy Spirit, apply the living and active Word of God to my heart and life today. I give you permission to do your eternal work in me and through me.

DAY 343

*I Peter 2:5 Ye also, as **lively stones**, are built up **a spiritual house**, **an holy priesthood**, to offer up spiritual sacrifices, acceptable to God by Jesus Christ.*

As a living spiritual house, a holy priesthood, we are to dedicate ourselves to the work of Jesus Christ above all else. This involves the sacrifice of praise—Psalm 27:6; prayer – Psalm 141:2; and a spirit yielded to Him—Psalm 51:17. God is careful to remind us that no part of our being is excluded as a living sacrifice—Romans 12:1. It is our reasonable service.

Father God, You are more than worthy of any sacrifice I am able to offer today. I know you have given me all that is required to be a lively stone in your spiritual house. I present my body, soul, and spirit to you today as a living sacrifice. It is only reasonable considering your own sacrifice for me.

DAY 344

*I Peter 2:9 But ye are a **chosen generation**, a **royal priesthood**, an **holy nation**, a **peculiar people**; that ye should shew forth the praises of him who hath called you out of darkness into his marvellous light...*

Notice what our Lord has made us—a chosen generation, a royal priesthood, a holy nation, a peculiar people. Why He has done so—that His light, His glory, and grace would be readily seen in and through us.

Lord, you could have chosen anything to show forth your glory. You could have written it in the stars, you could have ordained angels to sing your praises from the heavens day and night so that all the earth could hear; instead you chose me. May I live worthy of that high calling.

DAY 345

*I Peter 2:10 Which in time past were not a people, but are **now the people of God**: which had not obtained mercy, but **now have obtained mercy**.*

The Children of Israel were given the responsibility of presenting and promoting God's glory to the rest of the world. Because of Israel's unbelief and disobedience, the church has now obtained mercy to carry out that all-important directive. Jesus prayed for us to be united in this effort so that the world would believe (John 17:20 – 23). Will you be an answer to His prayer today?

O righteous Father, I have beheld your glory and have known love that is unique to your children. Help me to make your Name known in my corner of the world this day.

200

DAY 346

*I Peter 2:24 Who his own self bare our sins in his own body on the tree, that we, **being dead to sins, should live unto righteousness: by whose stripes ye were healed**.*

Life from death—creation is full of examples: A seed falling to the ground to produce new life, the barren branches of winter waking in spring with stunning blossoms and green leaves, a mother dying to self to give life to her child. All intended to picture the death of One who created in order that His creation could experience genuine life.

Jesus, thank you once again for your enormous sacrifice which brought us abundant life. Help me today to die to self in order to give life to others.

DAY 347

*I Peter 3:18 For Christ also hath once suffered for sins, the just for the unjust, **that he might bring us to God**, being put to death in the flesh, but quickened by the Spirit…*

I have been brought to God, to a place where I can commune with the Holy One. How did I get here? I did not have the required credentials, name, wardrobe, or relationship. However, the mystery of all mysteries is that these things were showered upon me by One who had it all. For me to come, He had to lay it all down.

Jesus, you gave all you had because I had nothing to give. May I too be quickened by your Spirit as I die to my flesh.

DAY 348

*I Peter 4:14 If ye be reproached for the name of Christ, happy are ye; for **the spirit of glory and of God resteth upon you**: on their part he is evil spoken of, but on your part he is glorified.*

Have you been suffering because of your commitment to Christ? Count it all joy, beloved. What would seem oppression has been overruled by the Spirit and is now an opportunity for you to show forth His glory.

It is only by the presence and power of your Spirit that the proof of my faith, though tested by fire, may be found to result in praise, glory, and honor as you, Christ, are revealed in my life.

DAY 349

*II Peter 1:3 According as his divine power **hath given unto us all things that pertain unto life and godliness,** through the knowledge of him that hath called us to glory and virtue…*

We have it already! Everything we need to live an abundant and godly life has come with the indwelling of the Holy Spirit. We need not ask for the Lord to give us patience, kindness, goodness, gentleness, etc., but to teach us to deny the flesh and put to use what has already been showered upon us.

Of your fullness we have all received grace upon grace. Since you have given me all that I need for life and godliness, help me to draw upon those blessings today making others thirsty for the same provision.

DAY 350

*II Peter 1:4 Whereby are given unto us exceeding great and precious promises: that by these ye might be **partakers of the divine nature**, **having escaped the corruption that is in the world through lust.***

Satan's plan is to trap us with the lust of the flesh, the lust of the eyes, and the boastful pride of life. If, however, we will cling to and apply the exceeding great and precious promises God has given in His Word, we can escape those corruptions and allow the glory of the risen Lord to shine in and through us.

Lord, it is my desire to appropriate your great and precious promises today. When I am tempted either by the enemy or by my own fleshly desires, I trust you will shine the light of your word upon my heart and pierce through any darkness so that I may remain sensitive to your leading.

DAY 351

*I John 1:1-3 That which was from the beginning, which we have heard, which we have seen with our eyes, which we have looked upon, and our hands have handled, of the Word of life; ² (For the life was manifested, and we have seen it, and bear witness, and shew unto you that eternal life, which was with the Father, and was manifested unto us;) ³ That which we have seen and heard declare we unto you, that ye also may have fellowship with us: **and truly our fellowship is with the Father, and with his Son Jesus Christ.***

Fellowship involves a common bond or mutual interest with others. We share a commonality with our brothers and sisters in Christ since we have all been brought near to the

Father through the work of the Son. Fellowship also involves sharing of joys, interests, sufferings, and sorrows. How is your fellowship with other believers? And more importantly, how is your fellowship with the Father?

Father, I have often neglected the fellowship which you desire to have with your children. I read in your Word that you experience compassion, anger, grief, joy, and even sorrow. May your interests be my interests this day.

DAY 352

*I John 1:4 And these things write we unto you, **that your joy may be full**.*

Fullness of joy is the Father's desire for His children. Jesus tells His disciples that such will come from abiding in His love (John 15:11), and as a result of asking for anything in His name (John 16:24). Our joy meter measures maximum levels when fellowship with the Lord is at priority status.

Abiding in your love and walking in your truth indeed brings that sweet communion that you describe as fullness of joy. I would have never known the fullness if I had not at once been empty. Pour your living water through me today.

DAY 353

*I John 2:26, 27 These things have I written unto you concerning them that seduce you. [27] But **the anointing which ye have received of him abideth in you**, and ye need not that any man teach you: but as the same anointing teacheth you of all things, and is truth, and is no lie, and even as it hath taught you, ye shall abide in him.*

We need to be very careful from whom we receive instruction. All God's truth will line up with the full counsel of God's Word and will be confirmed by the Holy Spirit who resides within each believer. God is delighted to confirm His Word in your life today.

Father, how thankful I am that you have given us the Spirit of Truth. As I abide in you, I trust that you will help me to quickly recognize any spirit of error. Sanctify me in truth, Lord; your Word is truth

DAY 354

I John 4:4 **Ye are of God**, *little children, and* **have overcome them**: *because* **greater is he that is in you, than he that is in the world.**

Notice the tense of the verb in this passage. You "have" overcome. It has already been accomplished *for* you and therefore will be accomplished *in* you. If the Sovereign of the universe is ruling in your heart, you will overcome because He has overcome.

You know, Lord, every circumstance I will face today, tomorrow, and the day after. May your resurrection power be unhindered and unleashed in and through your servant this day.

DAY 355

I John 4:5, 6 They are of the world: therefore speak they of the world, and the world heareth them. ⁶ **We are of God**: *he that knoweth God heareth us; he that is not of God heareth not us. Hereby know we the spirit of truth, and the spirit of error.*

Who is most interested in what you have to say? Are you tickling the ears of the world? The Word of God is as a sword piercing through darkness. The lust of the flesh, the lust of the eyes and the boastful pride of life will bristle against it. Our directive is to speak the truth in love, pray it in, and live it out allowing the Holy Spirit to do His transforming work.

Spirit of Truth, speak to me and through me today even if it is uncomfortable. Use that blessed double-edged sword to do your transforming work and let it begin in me.

DAY 356

I John 4:11, 12 Beloved, if God so loved us, we ought also to love one another. [12] No man hath seen God at any time. **If we love one another, God dwelleth in us, and his love is perfected in us.**

Is it a sacrifice to love those whom God has asked you to love today? He understands. His love was also a sacrifice. Are you willing to be crucified with Christ so that His life can be revealed in you?

Lord, thank you for reminding me that I am not always easy to love, and yet you continue to do so. Channel your love through me today.

DAY 357

I John 4:13 Hereby know we that we dwell in him, and he in us, because **he hath given us of his Spirit.**

The God who created this universe and all things in it desires to dwell in His creation, not in trees, flowers, and the animals that roam the earth; but in you and me. Can you grasp the enormity of that? You will know His presence when you are able to love the unlovable, have joy in the midst of difficult circumstances, experience peace that passes understanding, let your forbearing spirit be known to all men, show kindness to those who are unkind, goodness to those who have used you, gentleness to the harsh, and exhibit self control in all things.

Lord, I confess that I do not always want to be loving, full of joy, patient, peaceful, kind, good, gentle, and self controlled, but I do sense your Spirit desiring to be all this through me. I submit myself to your indwelling power today.

DAY 358

I John 5:4 For **whatsoever is born of God overcometh the world***: and this is the victory that overcometh the world, even our faith.*

Faith in God and His victory through Jesus Christ is the key to every kind of triumph in your life. Whether it is a spiritual, physical, mental, or emotional struggle, Jesus has already conquered it. Will you fight with your own strength or the power of His might?

You have given me the opportunity to participate in your victory. Some trust in chariots and some trust in horses, but I will trust in the name of the LORD my God.

DAY 359

I John 5:11-13 And this is the record, that God hath given to us eternal life, and this life is in his Son. [12] **He that hath the**

Son hath life*; and he that hath not the Son of God hath not life. [13] These things have I written unto you that believe on the name of the Son of God; that ye may know that ye have eternal life, and that ye may believe on the name of the Son of God.*

God breathed these powerful and encouraging words through John so that there would be no doubt that if we have received God's Son we have also received eternal life. We may be workers in the church, givers to charity, and studiers of the Scripture, but if we have said, "No" to Jesus Christ and all that His name encompasses, we have said no to eternal life.

What a gift! Life eternal in Jesus Christ. You are Savior, Lord, Master, Owner, Prophet, Priest, and King of Kings. You are the Prince of Peace, Mighty God, Creator, and Sustainer. You are the Exalted One, the Risen One, the Beginning, and the End. You are Wisdom and Knowledge and my best friend. Yes, Yes, as long as I have breath, I say yes to you as my Lord.

DAY 360

I John 5:14, 15 And this is the confidence that we have in him, that, **if we ask any thing according to his will, he heareth us:** *[15] And if we know that he hear us, whatsoever we ask, we know that we have the petitions that we desired of him*

What is the prayer that always receives a yes? "Thy will be done." How do I know if my petitions are according to His will? I must learn of His character, His ways, and His promises through His Word, then by prayer, supplications, and thanksgiving let my request be made know to Him. As I seek Him, I will find Him when I search for Him with all my heart.

Father, you alone know what is best for those I intercede on behalf of including myself. As I bring my petitions before you, remind me of your words concerning each circumstance. As I delight myself in you, I trust that the desires of my heart will be the desires of your heart also.

DAY 361

*I John 5:20 And we know that the Son of God is come, **and hath given us an understanding, that we may know him that is true, and we are in him that is true**, even in his Son Jesus Christ. This is the true God, and eternal life.*

Would you like to have all the treasures of wisdom and knowledge? According to Colossians 2:3 these treasures are hidden in Christ Jesus. When you know Him and are in Him, you have it all. If you get anything in this life, be sure to get Wisdom avoiding the way that seems right to man—the way of death.

I know that you have come and have given me understanding so that I can know truth—know you. Help me, Lord, to apply all the treasures of wisdom and knowledge made available to me.

DAY 362

*II John 1:2 For **the truth's sake, which dwelleth in us, and shall be with us for ever**.*

What truth dwells in us and is with us forever? Jesus—the Way, the Truth and the Life. The Spirit is truth and guides us into the truth of God's Holy Word. Jesus prayed that we would be sanctified in this truth. Praise Him today for the eternal, triune gift of truth.

As I rejoice in the truth, Lord, I rejoice in you. May your abundant truth be manifested in my life today.

DAY 363

Jude 1: Jude, the servant of Jesus Christ, and brother of James, **to them that are sanctified by God the Father, and preserved in Jesus Christ, and called...**

Throughout the past, present, and future the entire Godhead has been and will continue to be involved in your salvation. The Holy Spirit called you unto salvation—past tense. You are sanctified by the Father—present tense. And Jesus Christ preserves you for your future home in glory. Praise Father Son and Holy Ghost!

You have called me to yourself; you have set me apart and begun a good work in me. I trust that you will complete that work and make me fit for your kingdom. How thankful I am for your keeping power, Lord Jesus!

DAY 364

Revelation 5:9, 10 And they sung a new song, saying, Thou art worthy to take the book, and to open the seals thereof: for thou wast slain, and hast redeemed us to God by thy blood out of every kindred, and tongue, and people, and nation; [10] And **hast made us unto our God kings and priests: and we shall reign on the earth.**

The everlasting life that God has given to us includes great responsibility as well as great joy. The training begins now as we allow Christ to be King and Priest in us and through us.

You are worthy, O Lord, to reign not only in the spiritual and physical realm, but most of all in my life. Take your place on the throne. I submit myself to your will!

DAY 365

*Romans 8:28 And we know that all things work together for good to them that love God, to them who are the **called according to his purpose**.*

This became my father's life verse after breaking his neck in a diving accident and becoming a quadriplegic while serving in the United States Air Force. I witnessed the power of God's Word played out in his life, seeing it tried and proven. For twenty-seven years my mother cared for Dad, and I also witnessed God's powerful Word living and active in her. She never complained, just consistently loved him and three girls with God's strength eclipsing her own. At the time of this writing I am caring for my mother who is terminal with bone cancer. Once again, the living active Word of God ministers through the power of the Holy Spirit to those who are called according to His purpose.

Every detail of Your Word, Lord, is tried and proven. Thank you for calling me according to your purpose, putting your love within me, and working all things for our good and your glory. Be magnified in my life today!

I pray that you have been blessed to discover who you are in Christ, realizing that He knows you and loves you deeper than you can fully comprehend on this side of eternity. One day, however, your eyes will be opened and you will know even as you are known:

*Revelation 2:17 He that hath an ear, let him hear what the Spirit saith unto the churches; To him that overcometh will I give to eat of the hidden manna, and will give him a white stone, and in the stone **a new name written, which no man knoweth saving he that receiveth it.***

FEAR NOT; HE KNOWS YOUR NAME!

Appendix A
Daily Armor

Jehovah Sabaoth, Lord of Hosts, you have commanded me to be strong in the power of your might, to put on your full armor that I may be able to stand firm against the schemes of the devil.

I realize that even though it seems like I am fighting against flesh and blood, my struggle is not against flesh and blood, but against the rulers, against the powers, against the world forces of darkness, and against the spiritual forces of wickedness in the heavenly places.

Therefore, I take up the full armor you have provided for me:

I am thankful, Father, for the **helmet of salvation** that was purchased by the blood of my Lord Jesus Christ. I know without the shedding of blood there is no remission of sin. Because the blood of Christ was shed for and applied to me, I am free from the power of sin in my life. As I wear this helmet, I set my mind on you, Lord, so that I can remain in perfect peace.

I wear my **breastplate of righteousness** most humbly with full knowledge that I am a new creature in Christ; old things are passed away and all things are become new. Thank you, Jesus, for the exchange of robes as we entered into covenant— my filthy rags for your righteousness—what a gift!

I put on the **belt of truth** knowing that it is necessary in order to keep all my other armor in place. Jesus, you are the truth, your Word is truth, and I must filter all that comes into my life by your living and powerful Word. Give me wisdom and discernment for this day.

Speaking of your Word, I take up the **sword of the Spirit**. It is with this living and active sword through which you pierce even the toughest of characters and judge the thoughts and intentions of my own heart. Just as Jesus used this sword against the enemy in the wilderness, I claim the power that is available also to me to defeat Satan and his adversaries when they approach; they shall not apprehend one who is fully prepared.

My **shield of faith** is fully soaked in the water of your Word so as to quench all the fiery darts of the evil one. Bring to my memory, Holy Spirit, all that you have taught me; and as I spend time with my Father today, prepare me for whatever trials I will face. When those arrows come, help me to quickly find the passages in the Holy Scriptures that apply so that I will not be burned. I want absolutely no chink in my armor.

I ask you to help me shod my feet with the preparation of the **gospel of peace**. As much as is possible, it is my desire to live at peace with all men. I realize, however, that compromising my faith in you or your Word will not bring peace to any situation. What good news you have brought to mankind! May I never be afraid to toss the lifeline to those who are drowning in the sea of despair.

Jesus, as I stand here fully covered, I know that I have just dressed up in you. You are Salvation, you are my Righteousness, you are Truth, and you are Peace. You are the Living Word, you are my Shield, and my Protector; my faith is in you. You are my all, my everything.

Now I am on the alert and ready to pray in the Spirit with all perseverance and petition for all the saints.

Identity Prayer

Father God, you are holy and righteous and worthy of all praise. You are the God who sees me, who knows me and continues to love me with an unconditional everlasting love. You are my Creator and Sustainer. Thank you for the identity you have given me as a child of the King. I confess with my mouth and with my actions that I have been given all things pertaining to life and godliness, I am an able minister of the new covenant, an ambassador of Christ, and accepted in the Beloved.

Thank you for blessing me with every spiritual blessing in heavenly places and reminding me often that I am a beloved child of the King, called into fellowship with Jesus Christ, chosen in Him, crucified with Christ and comforted of God.

It is my desire to live as one who is dead to sin but alive to God in Christ Jesus. You have made me an epistle of Christ that your Gospel might be circulated through me making a permanent impression on the lives of others.

I am forgiven and free, a fellow citizen of the Kingdom, filled with the fruits of righteousness. I have not been given a spirit of fear but of power, love, and a sound mind. I will stand firm in the freedom Christ purchased for me and not be subject again to a yoke of bondage.

I am a house of Christ, part of the holy priesthood, and an heir according to the promise. I am your workmanship created in Christ Jesus for good works which God prepared beforehand that I should walk in them. I am hidden with Christ in God.

When Christ who is my life is revealed then I will also be revealed with Him in glory.

Since I have been justified by faith I have peace with God through my Lord Jesus Christ. You know me, Lord, like no one else. How thankful I am that you understand my thoughts from afar and are intimately acquainted with all my ways. Search me, try me, show me my hurtful ways, and make clear to me the things that are of eternal value.

I am a laborer together with you, Lord, desiring that my motivation will always be a sincere love for you, so as not to produce wood, hay and stubble, but gold, silver and precious stones.

You gave me the ministry of reconciliation when I was made nigh by the blood of Christ. Not only am I a new creation, but I am more than a conqueror through Him who loved me. I choose to not only stand my ground against the enemy today but to gain some ground for you in the process of my trials.

It is my desire to walk as an obedient child and a partaker of Christ which may be peculiar to the world but glorifying to you.

Today I am quickened, raised, and renewed. The more I become what you created me to be the less I will resemble the old lump of clay.

Not only do you call me salt and light, but you have made me a saved, sealed saint, sanctified and strengthened to be a sweet savor of my Savior.

I am a holy temple, triumphant in Christ, and taught of God. I have been saved to the uttermost, made a vessel of mercy and a vessel of honor. May I continue to be the witness you desire, yoked together with Christ and zealous for good deeds.

.

CPSIA information can be obtained
at www.ICGtesting.com
Printed in the USA
LVOW08s0255080917
547863LV00001B/1/P